THE BOOK OF
St Andrews

THE BOOK OF
St Andrews

Edited by Robert Crawford

Polygon

First published in paperback in 2007 by Polygon
an imprint of Birlinn Ltd

West Newington House
10 Newington Road
Edinburgh
EH9 1QS
www.birlinn.co.uk

First published in 2005

10-digit ISBN 1 904598 99 4
13-digit ISBN 978 1 90498 99 2

British Library Cataloguing-in-Publication Data
A catalogue record for this book is available on request from
the British Library

Designed and typeset by StudioLR
Printed and bound by Creative Print and Design, Abertillery, Wales

to

Jill Gamble

Sandra McDevitt

Frances Mullan

Jane Sommerville

whose work as secretaries
has made possible the making of this book

ACKNOWLEDGEMENTS

This book exists thanks to the practical support of the St Andrews Scottish Studies Centre, whose Director is Professor Douglas Dunn. In particular, I wish to thank the Centre's secretary, Mrs Frances Mullan, who prepared the typescript for publication, and kept track of its many electronic files. While editing this book I was Head of the School of English at the University of St Andrews, and it is a necessary pleasure to acknowledge the debt I owe to the School's secretaries, to whom the book is dedicated. I would also like to thank all my other colleagues for their friendship and support, and to extend gratitude to the staff of the University Library, not least its Special Collections department. St Andrews is where I live with my family, and I hope Alice, Lewis, and Blyth may enjoy this book. It does not repay the debt I owe them.

Hearty thanks are due to the many living writers who have given work to *The Book of St Andrews*, often on the most generous (which, in some cases, means non-existent) terms. The resourceful Nick Wetton helped clear copyright permissions, which are duly acknowledged. At Polygon, Hugh Andrew, Lilias Fraser, Siân Gibson, and Alison Rae were a pleasure to work with. Time now for a walk in the Lade Braes.

CONTENTS

Introduction

This anthology of imaginative writing is arranged like St Andrews itself, where you can find an Art Deco cinema, a late medieval spire, and a 1970s residential block all on the same street. The Book of St Andrews juxtaposes poems, stories and memoirs with scant regard to chronological order, but in the confidence that each contribution, lively in its own right, may also enhance the others. The anthology, like the town, contains golfers, kids from the caravan site, students and professors, born Fifers and visitors from near and far parts of the planet. Some contributors live and work in St Andrews; others passed through some time ago; one or two, like Homer or St Andrew, never saw the place, but are linked to it regardless.

Just as much of St Andrews itself was built relatively recently, so quite a lot of the writing here is new. Contemporary authors were asked to contribute work that related to St Andrews either tangentially or directly, and that might sit alongside celebrated St Andrews writings from the past – whether poems by Robert Fergusson, or Margaret Oliphant's ghost story 'The Library Window' (written when the university was debating whether or not to admit female students), or Andrew Lang's poem about his 'haunted town'. The anthology includes work produced in four different millennia, and for a number of today's writers, such as Sarah Hall, A. L. Kennedy, Paul Muldoon, and Seamus Heaney, St Andrews remains a place haunted, sometimes even scarred, by the past – a 'Reformation bombsite', in Les Murray's memorable phrase. But the new work made for this book also suggests by its very existence that St Andrews is a point of fresh growth, a big village where remarkable and unexpected things can happen at the drop of a hat.

Miles beyond the end of the railway line, a tiny town containing one of Europe's senior universities, part of its grassy coastline celebrated round the world as the *fons et origo* of golf, St Andrews is an almost impossible place. Its assets are unique and improbable. Despite its size, it has its own castle and cathedral, theatre and galleries, pier, pubs and Poetry House. In this northern speck, over the centuries, the contested identity of Scotland has been made manifest. Pilgrims trekked here in the Middle Ages; Robert the Bruce prayed in its great cathedral; the Scottish Reformation tore the place apart, and people were burned alive in its streets; later, suffragettes set light to some of its buildings, and, during the decline and fall of the British Empire, 'retired pro-consuls', as Willa Muir puts it, 'were heard in loud voices referring to the townsfolk as "the natives"'. Since at least the eighteenth-century, when Robert Fergusson (Robert Burns's favourite Scottish poet) was a St Andrews student, the place has been involved in arguments about the Anglicization of Scottish culture. The languages used regularly in St Andrews have included Gaelic and Latin, Scots, English and French, not to mention other tongues such as the Polish of the exiles who came here at the time of the Second World War, some returning to Poland to fight in the Warsaw Uprising, others going to America or settling in St Andrews itself. There is a Polish inscription in one of the St Andrews public parks, and the Town Hall mosaic made by Polish soldier-artists is but one emblem of the town's internationalism. In the 1930s, though none of today's blue plaques announces the fact, St Andrews was an important site on the map of Scottish cultural and political nationalism, a meeting place for writers, artists and composers whose outlook was both nationalist and internationally alert; in the 1970s, in rather different circumstances, it nurtured several influential thinkers of the political right. In the twenty-first century St Andrews is more cosmopolitan than ever, but also more inclusively and resolutely Scottish, a place that, however small, has set its face against Anglophobia and Little Scotlandism. It is, like its nation, independent-minded. It can seem smug and thrawnly parochial, but is also nimble and adaptable, a site of ambitious antiquity where the future can be dreamed and invented. That is one reason why it has been so attractive to writers, of whom St Andrews, over the last six centuries at least, has educated or played host to more than its fair share.

True, the place has disgraced itself. In 1746, just after the Battle of

Culloden, the university made the young 'Butcher' Cumberland its Chancellor, and a little over half a century later the poet and orientalist John Leyden thought the town 'for dancing, cards, golf, scandal, and drunkenness almost the capital of Scotland'. Yet this was also the era when the university awarded an honorary degree to Benjamin Franklin, when its student James Wilson helped shape the American Declaration of Independence, and when Dr Johnson considered the town 'eminently adapted to study and education'. Again, if the twentieth century saw the writers Willa and Edwin Muir and the American Scottish nationalist James H. Whyte cold-shouldered by the snootier members of the community, it also saw the later founding in St Andrews of Scotland's Poetry Festival, St Anza, and the appointment of a number of leading writers to the permanent staff of the university's School of English. Sometimes the place gets things right.

Other anthologies could be made about St Andrews. They might focus on historical records; on golf; on religion; on travellers; on the politics of academia. Though this book touches on all of these, its distinctive focus is on St Andrews as a place of the literary imagination: windswept enough to be thoroughly convincing, but sufficiently unhassled to let imaginations flourish. So as not to interrupt the flow of imaginative writing with an archipelago of notes, I have put all information about the writers at the back of this book, alphabetically arranged after the poems and stories. Just to break the rules, I have included a scattering of non-fiction by writers with imaginative gifts – from John Knox to Kay Redfield Jamison, and from Dr Johnson to Ian Rankin. On the whole, I have avoided taking chapters out of novels, though I was tempted by such works as John Buchan's *The Free Fishers* (whose hero is a St Andrews professor of belles-lettres) and Val McDermid's *The Distant Echo* (in which a dead body is discovered on Hallowhill). Still, this anthology does have its share of corpses and professors. Thanks to Roddy Lumsden, Andrew Lang and Meaghan Delahunt, there is too – how could there not be? – a tincture of golf.

Also included are Liz Lochhead on croquet, Kathleen Jamie on curlews, and Douglas Young on a shot hoopoe. If I have included too much of my own work, this should be taken partly as sheer egotism, and partly as an expression of love for the place where I have lived and worked for the last sixteen years. I hope you encounter in what follows surprises ancient and modern, and that, whether you read as an intimate of St Andrews or as a total stranger, you find enjoyable things in *The Book of St Andrews*.

R.C.
Castle House / The Poetry House
2005

GAVIN DOUGLAS

Storme Wyntre

from *The Prolog of the Sevynt Buik of Eneados* (early sixteenth century)

Widequhair with fors so Eolus schouttis schyll	*everywhere; shrill*
In this congelyt sessioune scharp and chyll,	*frozen season*
The callour air, penetrative and puire,	*fresh; pure*
Dasyng the bluide in every creature,	*numbing*
Maid seik warm stovis, and beyne fyris hoyt,	*seek; pleasant*
In double garmont cled and wyly coyt,	*undercoat*
Wyth mychty drink, and meytis confortive,	*[comforting food]*
Agayne the storme wyntre for to strive.	

KAY REDFIELD JAMISON

The Indian Summer of My Life

St Andrews, my tutor was saying, was the only place he knew where it snowed horizontally. An eminent neurophysiologist, he was a tall, lanky, and droll Yorkshireman who, like many of his fellow English, believed that rather superior weather, to say nothing of civilization, ended where the Scottish countryside began. He had a point about the weather. The ancient, grey-stoned town of St Andrews sits right on the North Sea and takes blasts of late-autumn and winter winds that have to be experienced to be believed. I had been living in Scotland for several months by that time, and I had become a definite believer. The winds were especially harsh just off the town's East Sands, where the university's marine biology laboratory had been built.

There were ten or so of us third-year zoology students, and we were sitting, shivering, wool layered, wool gloved, and teeth chattering, in the damp cold of the tank-filled laboratory. My tutor seemed even more puzzled by my being in these advanced zoology courses than I was.

He was an authority on what one might have thought was a somewhat specialized portion of the animal kingdom, namely the auditory nerve of the locust, and just prior to his remarks about horizontal snowfalls in Scotland he had put my striking ignorance of zoological matters out into the public domain.

The task at hand was to set up electrophysiological recordings from the locust's auditory nerve; the rest of the students – all of whom had been specializing in science for many years – had already, and neatly, dissected out the necessary tidbits of bug and were duly recording away. I hadn't any idea what I was doing, my tutor knew this, and I was wondering yet again why the university had placed me at this level of science studies. I had gotten as far as picking out the locust from his cage – because it was kept warm, I prolonged my stay in the insect room for a rather lingering time – and had finally narrowed down its body regions into wings, body, and head. This was not going to get me very far. I felt my tutor's tall presence behind me and turned to see a sardonic smile on his face. He went to the chalkboard, drew what certainly looked to be a locust, circled a region on the animal's head, and said in his most elaborate accent, 'For your edification, Miss Jamison, he-ah is the e-ah'; the class roared, so did I, and I reconciled myself to a year of being truly and hopelessly behind – I was; but I learned a lot, and had great fun as I did so. (My laboratory notes for the locust experiment reflect my early recognition that I was in over my head; after detailing the experimental method in my lab report – 'The head, wings, and legs were removed from a locust. After exposing the air sacs by cutting the metathoracic sternites, the auditory nerve was located and cut centrally to exclude the possibility of responses from the cerebral ganglion,' and so on – the write-up ended with 'Due to a misunderstanding of instructions, and a general lack of knowledge about what was going on, a broader range of pitch stimulation was not tested and, by the time the misunderstanding was understood, the auditory nerve was fatigued. So was I.')

There were, however, definite advantages to studying invertebrate zoology. For starters, unlike in psychology, you could eat your subjects. The lobsters – fresh from the sea and delicious – were especially popular. We cooked them in beakers over Bunsen burners until one of our lecturers, remarking that 'It has not gone unnoticed that some of your subjects seem to be letting themselves out of their tanks at night,' put a halt to our attempts to supplement college meals.

That year I walked for long hours along the sea and through the town and sat for hours mulling and writing among the ancient ruins of the city. I never tired of imagining what the twelfth-century cathedral must once have been, what glorious stained glass must once have filled its now-empty stone-edged windows; nor could I escape the almost archetypal pullings of Sunday services in the college chapel, which, like the university itself, had been built during the early fifteenth century. The medieval traditions of learning and religion were threaded together in a deeply mystifying and wonderful way. The thick scarlet gowns of the undergraduates, said to be brightly coloured because of an early Scottish king's decree that students, as potentially dangerous to the State, should be easily recognized, brought vivid contrast to the grey buildings of the town; and, after chapel, the red-gowned students would walk to the end of the town's pier, further extending their vivid contrast to the dark skies and the sea.

It was, it is, a mystical place: full of memories of cold, clear nights and men and women in evening dress, long gloves, silk scarves, kilts, and tartan sashes over the shoulders of women in elegant floor-length silk gowns; an endless round of formal balls; late dinner parties of salmon, hams, fresh game, sherry, malt whiskies, and port; bright scarlet gowns on the backs of students on bicycles, in dining and lecture halls, in gardens, and on the ground as picnic blankets in the spring. There were late nights of singing and talking with my Scottish roommates; long banks of daffodils and bluebells on the hills above the sea; seaweed and rocks and limpet shells along the yellow, high-tided sands, and ravishingly beautiful Christmas services at the end of term:

undergraduates in their long, bright gowns of red, and graduate students in their short, black sombre ones; the old and beautiful carols; hanging lamps of gold-chained crowns, and deeply carved wooden choir stalls; the recitation of lessons in both the English public school and the far gentler, more lyrical Scottish accents. Leaving the chapel late that winter night was to enter onto an ancient scene, the sight of scarlet against snow, the ringing of bells, and a clear, full moon.

St Andrews provided a gentle forgetfulness over the preceding painful years of my life. It remains a haunting and lovely time to me, a marrow experience. For one who during her undergraduate years was trying to escape an inexplicable weariness and despair, St Andrews was an amulet against all manner of longing and loss, a year of gravely held but joyous remembrances. Throughout and beyond a long North Sea winter, it was the Indian summer of my life.

WILLIAM DRUMMOND OF HAWTHORNDEN

Parliament Hall

from *Epigrams, xxxix*

S. Andrew, why does thou giue up thy Schooles,
And Bedleme turne, and parlament house of fooles?

Andreapolis

Urbs sacra, nuper eras toti venerabilis orbi,
    Nec fuit in toto sanctior orbe locus.
Iuppiter erubuit tua cernens templa, sacello
    Et de Tarpeio multa querela fuit.
Haec quoque contemplans Ephesinae conditor aedis,
    Ipse suum merito risit et odit opus.
Vestibus aequabant templorum marmora mystae,
    Cunctaque divini plena nitoris erant.
Ordinis hic sacri princeps, spectabilis auro,
    Iura dabat patribus Scotia quotquot habet.
Priscus honor periit; traxerunt templa ruinam,
    Nec superest mystis qui fuit ante nitor:
Sacra tamen Musis urbs es, Phoebique ministris,
    Nec maior meritis est honor ille tuis.
Lumine te blando, Musas quae diligit, Eos
    Adspicit, et roseis molliter afflat equis.
Mane novo iuxta Musarum murmurat aedes
    Rauca Thetis, somnos et iubet esse breves.
Proximus est campus, studiis hic fessa iuventus
    Se recreat, vires sumit et inde novas.
Phocis amor Phoebi fuit olim, Palladis Acte:
    In te iam stabilem fixit uterque larem.

St Andrews

translated by Robert Crawford from the Latin of Arthur Johnston (1587–1641)

Sacred St Andrews, the whole wide world
Saw you as the burgh of God.
Jove, eyeing your great Cathedral,
Blushed for his own wee Tarpeian kirk.
The architect of the Ephesian temple,
Seeing yours, felt like a fake.
Culdee priests in holy cassocks
Gazed through your East Neuk of light.
St Andrews' Archbishop, clad in gold,
Bellowed at Scotland's Parliament.
Now that's gone, walls ankle-high,
Priestly *fiat lux* tarnished.
Still you pull poets, though. You wow
Lecturers and lab technicians.
Aurora of the Peep o' Day in Fife
Frisks ashore with salt-reddened fingers,
Herring-sparkle of dawn.
Thetis coughs through 10 a.m. haar,
Waking hirpling, hungover students
Who sober up with golfclubs.
Phocis was Phoebus's long-time lover,
Attica of Pallas. In St Andrews
Each dances. Forever. Now.

SEAMUS HEANEY

To the Poets of St Andrews
adapted from the lost original 'Ut in Lusitania olim miles ...'
attributed to Arthur Johnston (1587–1641)

As when in Lusitania once the legions
Stood under halted standards by Lima River
And refused to wade across the water north
To make war on the clans because the clans
Had spread a rumour that Lethe flowed to Ocean
By way of those clear, gravel-chattering fords
And silent bends, one veteran commander
(To show this was no bourne of forgetfulness)
Splashed into the shallows and kept going
Under his campaign gear, his spear-shaft firm
As his grasp on memory when he'd got across
And started to call back name after Roman name
Of his sweltering comrades,

         So I
Who instead of spear-shaft grasp my crummock
And step wet from a ferry south of Forth
Recall your poets' names, in wind-borne Latin
Ut in Lusitania olim miles ...

Irresistible

I didn't understand this, but then I lost him and I learned; the dead steal everything, even the Spring. The stretch in your days, waking early to light, new hungers, blossoms, speed – if you don't stop them, they'll fumble over all of that, until it's greasy and their own. So the year will break forward, open, spread, but you can't have it, can't be alone with it, because of them: the greedy dead.

Which is why security concerns me, why I'm careful and take pains. There's nothing of his in my house, which is a house he never saw, and my hair's a different colour, usually red, and I've moved into a town we didn't know and I don't watch the films that he enjoyed and I have discipline and rules that stop reminders, lock off any pathways past my guard. But everyone knows the Spring is tricky, makes you weak.

And it's here again, of course, the seasonal, irresistible welcome home for nothing I want. I have never insisted on seeing the green start of leaves, or the quickened birds, or the sown fields changed by every morning. I would rather avoid the comfort in my spine that comes with heat, the beginning of heat, life clear in it as the reach of a hand, as breath. The world returned without him – I don't need another proof of that. And I've already accepted there's a part of me that's fallen, won't be reclaimed.

I know I am not entirely myself.

Not when the Spring makes me expect him.

Not when he still hurts in my skin.

Fuck him.

An absence should be more absent. A word should have meaning – gone meaning gone.

Today he interfered before breakfast, caught me half asleep. I was in the kitchen and looking for something: a jar, a bowl, I don't recall: and I opened up this cupboard and inside was a mass of whitish tendrils, like braced legs, a suggestion of predatory insects, or disease. I dropped my coffee cup, broke it: the coffee everywhere and hot while I'm working out that I've simply forgotten a bag of potatoes and, Spring seeping up to wake them, they have sprouted, bolted in the dark. My fault – I'm becoming untidy and should do better.

The trouble is, I'm more susceptible after shocks. When I made another coffee, shaking slightly, in he slipped; because while we were courting – and we even liked to call it that, the old-fashioned word, courting – while we were courting, I used to shake. I'd hear him on the phone and shiver: a mild, involuntary type of thing. I tended to tremble when we kissed. Talking and meeting and having that heart-shocked, rooftop feeling, that first sweet terror of love: describing each other to each other, finding ourselves out, as if we had never been seen before: the mouth, the eyes, the rush to know, to say our names and make us real – it can be difficult to forget how well we started.

And this morning I had the scent of him in the kitchen, just enough to fool my pulse before the traces thinned away and I was left to deal with the usual weeping. I also had to go upstairs and shower, wash off the feel of resurrected flesh.

Naturally, he picks a Sunday to attack, the undefended blank in anybody's week. I stayed in bed until eleven to cut the whole thing short, but there are still hours of this to grind through before Monday and my chance to leave for work.

I could almost nip into the office this afternoon, turn off the alarm and type some letters, anticipate phone calls that won't come, spin and glide in my nicely supportive, adjustable chair. Before him, I would have hated this – photocopying, filing, cakes for anniversaries and birthdays, chocolate on Fridays, lucky dip for Christmas presents, spending limit to be confirmed. So many kinds of dreadful fun. But my tastes have changed. Having seven people I can talk to between tasks and during lunch breaks, that's important. And at home I can share their television choices, note plot turns and weather forecasts for discussion the following day, memorise features involving children, holiday destinations, arguments. In this way I can justify my nights spent on the sofa, staring at colours and hearing noise and letting the warm, diluted world wash over me like milk

It would be eccentric, though, working on a Sunday. It would stand out and possibly lead to requests that I should explain myself.

And I am not myself, so I can't do that.

I can't really go shopping, either – not enough shops. It's hard even in the week: forcing chatter on some bored assistant to keep your mind at bay, or surrendering into that bleak slide of conversation, confessional snippets, unruly laughs – both of you strangers who meet too many strangers, who never talk to anyone who cares. Sometimes you can smell it on them, that glaze of misery, or sometimes their horror stays discrete until they speak. Either way, they'll be hopeful when they see you, ever after: they'll anticipate relief, give you that plaintive grimace when you can't oblige because you are occasionally stunted, shrinking, and another few words could wear you flat. In a larger town, I could avoid connections, there would be a comfortable degree of choice – but anywhere larger and he'll be waiting, because we both travelled too much.

I can't walk in the nearest city, because we were there together once, hunting for somewhere to eat, for treats we could take with us on the road. I can't drive along the mild curve of the estuary bridge, because I told him about it – after that time I passed through there alone. I can't pay my toll for crossing, because the whole process will fill the car with his old irritation, the way he could love being angry about the scramble for fugitive change and the cold air beating in and the grimy booths and paying what was due.

He didn't like to pay for anything. Out for the night, he'd buy a round early, while everyone was fresh and could pay attention. He'd make a fuss about it – no option too expensive and his voice loud at the bar, demanding – on behalf of other people, demanding – then he'd tiptoe back, bringing everything with him at once, all the glasses held together in one dangerous bouquet, licking over his hands. Setting it down would be delicate work, dramatic, sometimes earned him applause. But he'd spend no more after that. If it seemed he might have to, he'd start a quarrel and we'd leave.

Fuck him.

This is what happens: I think of my life, of unconnected items, and always he cuts in.

Which means it's time for me to take a walk: there's more chance I can dodge him if I move about.

So put on the scarf and hat he didn't buy me, the new coat he never met, and sneak out by the back door.

I should see to the garden here – it would occupy me, perhaps completely, but it's much too small to care about: a tiny box of whitewashed walls, some mossed-over grass and beds I never thought would have the energy to go so wrong. I will get it tarmaced, concreted. I will bury everything.

I swing the gate shut behind me, fasten the latch.

'I used to sing in a jazz choir.'

A student couple is wandering down Bridge Street ahead of me. They don't match yet. She uses his name a lot – Terry, Terry, Terry – but won't step in closer the way he tries to: breaking their pace and leaning near, having to lurch himself straight again, stay neat. Still, she asks about his choir and then they to and fro enquiries about music which they may or may not really like, may or may not think gives an impression of them which is mature and open-minded, intelligent, loveable. Neither of them wants to be trapped inside this topic – it's both too cerebral and too revealing – but they don't know each other well enough to change tack easily.

I follow them into South Street, aware that I could help: provide a new subject they could share. If I barged past them now and muttered, then sped off, affecting a limp: arm twitching: small signs of distress – they'd be glad of the diversion.

But I do no such thing; only track silently behind them and think of the point they'll both reach when they want to know less of themselves, forget. In this pairing, or any other, it won't matter: eventually, every love will teach its lover how to hide from it, ignore it, wish it undone.

I turn off and leave them be, make for the broken cathedral and the graveyard.

Which is a good place, I use it quite often: potter between the headstones, think of the memory weathering free from them. I imagine it fraying out into carelessness, carrying on the breeze until it's nothing: a vague chill, a tease of murmurs and then peace.

Someone's given the grass its first cut of the year and the taste of that is everywhere, sweet against tumbled masonry, the walls that have no purpose, the rooms of air. Not that I'm concerned with this – I come here for all the reminders of weight applied beneath the turf, the settlement of earth over the dead. I am surrounded by reliable interments, ones that did the job. Nobody could clamber up from anywhere like this, from any proper grave: they wouldn't have the strength.

Or that's the hopeful lie I tell myself. Another habit he bequeathed me, the practice of optimistic stupidity – along with searching the pockets of his coats, collecting him from bad addresses, spending dawns in the groggy dance of washing him and putting him to bed. Above all, though, was this practice of believing, of making his excuses credible.

I used to forgive him, because he seemed so consistently fragile. Although, actually he was the strongest man I knew. He truly did almost survive himself, every onslaught of his will. I'd catch its tick and twist inside the soft dark of his eyes, making its plans. And it would flicker up and watch me while he crouched and vomited, while he bled, while he messed himself, while he cried because he'd burned his fingers to the bone, numb drunk with a cigarette lit between them. It would be there when he cried for no reason, no visible pain, and there, too, when he screamed at me. It wanted me to hate him and it wanted him to hurt.

And in the end, that's what I wanted, too.

Fuck him.

For the poison dreams he'd have beside me, for the bitterness in his sweat, for the disappearances and insults, for killing someone that I loved – fuck him.

I'm starting to think of our last time at the hospital: the yellow way he looked, his missing tooth, his odd politeness with the panic underneath.

Can't have that, though – not today – so I begin to trot, go out of the grounds and on to the shore road, as if I am in a hurry, have a purpose.

Because I have – I want to watch the empty gulls: that smooth, pale cleverness in motion and calls that are nothing to do with me. You can waste hours with the gulls and no one will disturb you, unless another watcher maybe edges up and smiles in the nondescript way that implies shared admiration for nature and its works. Smiling back is possible, but then it isn't impolite to turn away again and study the rocks, the water, the circling birds.

Beyond this, I can take my pick of seafront hotels, little pubs. They've sopped up any number of Sundays with a quiet read at the papers in the lounge and pots of acrid tea and afterwards maybe a dinner: some kind of roast, boiled potatoes, other, harder vegetables, unsettling gravy. I never enjoy it, except for the part when I imagine that if I could ever be bothered to cook something like this for myself it would be better, it would be wholesome, it would be a welcome home.

I don't feel like a dinner today, though, and I would rather not be near a bar. Instead I keep walking over the rise and down and past the last hole of the golf course, then on to the heel of the sands. Nowhere else could cure me on a day like this.

This is where the sky comes down to you and scours across the strand, leads you along beside the water, the wide air catching you by the shoulders, cuffing the backs of your legs. You want it to make you blue and far away like the others already out here. You breath in the shine of salt and try to let your head drift, rest.

He loved to swim. Not a man for beaches, but avid in the water, a practised economy in his strokes. Started early, he used to tell me – gave himself larger shoulders than he might have otherwise and strong lungs and skills connected with life saving under various conditions.

And it is true that he didn't drown, not really.

I concentrate on the good hurt in my legs, the mild fight against instability underfoot. To my right is the white tear and fold of gentle surf and I slow, curve my track down to meet it and turn my back on the walkers, the joggers, the hand-in-handers, the families with children and happy dogs. I let the water lap my shoes – they're a pair I dislike – but I don't let it rise enough to wet my feet. The tide presses and sucks exactly as it would if I weren't here.

In the end I retreat, of course. I return to walking and what I miss.

Which isn't him, not precisely.

What I miss is being covered in him, the knowledge of him, I was always naked against that. And I was fully awake then and in true daylight, and seeing for two, living for two. I saved my life so I could say it to him. That was the best of being parted – our having so much to tell when we were back, when we were home, when we were still all right and our thoughts turned into facts, our perfect fact.

Who do I tell myself to now.

The beach stops in an ugly jumble of shore defences – spilled rock, wire cages filled with gravel, a scum of sea foam at their foot, yellow-stained. There's nowhere left to go.

I pause and stare at red flecks in the water, flutters of shadow, and then I can only go, re-cut my own track, face round towards the setting of the sun and let the dazzle watermark wherever else I look.

And I'm tired enough and sad enough and lonely enough to ask for this, so now I let myself remember our farewell visit, sitting in the plastic chair beside his bed and neither of us speaking.

He had the standard Formica cabinet, up by his head, but there was nothing on it: no presents, no cards, no signs that people worried for him and might want him to feel safe.

I didn't kiss him. I should have. Even shaking hands, that's a kind of goodbye, we could have done that. It was too late, though. So I just sat and he wiped his mouth, fingers unsteadied, tried brushing at his hair. He told me he'd be up and about soon, mentioned a number of days and then started crying.

I didn't cry, the part of me I'd used for feeling sad having rotted away, some time before. But I did know there wasn't enough of us left to be with any more. We were long gone. And the dead are meant to be alone – they try to get back, but they never can, not the way they want to.

I should have kissed him. That's a regret.

I'd let him know about it, if I could. I'd tell him everything, the whole of my time since we stopped, since my heart went still: the cold in every hour, the daily burial, the slow route I'll take to my house in this clean time of the evening, when the saved light will start rising from the watered sand, breathing up and bringing in the dark.

I should have kissed him.

ROBERT FERGUSSON

Elegy

On the Death of Mr DAVID GREGORY, *late Professor of Mathematics in the University of St Andrews*

Now mourn, ye college masters a'!
  And frae your ein a tear lat fa',   *eyes*
Fam'd *Gregory* death has taen awa'
  Without remeid;   *remedy*
The skaith ye've met wi's nae that sma', *harm*
  Sin Gregory's dead.

The students too will miss him sair,
To school them weel his eident care,   *diligent*
Now they may mourn for ever mair,
  They hae great need;
They'll hip the maist fek o' their lear, *skip most of their education*
  Sin Gregory's dead.

He could, by *Euclid*, prove lang sine
A ganging *point* compos'd a line;   *going/moving*
By numbers too he cou'd divine,
  Whan he did read,
That *three* times *three* just made up nine;
  But now he's dead.

In *Algebra* weel skill'd he was,
An' kent fu' well *proportion's* laws;
He cou'd make clear baith B's and A's
  Wi' his lang head;
Rin owr surd roots, but cracks or flaws; *Run; without*
  But now he's dead.

Weel vers'd was he in architecture,
An' kent the nature o' the *sector*,
Upon baith globes he weel cou'd lecture,
An' gar's tak heid;   *make us pay attention*
Of geometry he was the *hector*;
    But now he's dead.

Sae weel's he'd fley the students a',   *frighten*
Whan they war skelpin at the ba',   *making a noise*
They took leg bail and ran awa',   *flight from justice*
    Wi' pith and speid;
We winna get a sport sae braw
    Sin Gregory's dead.

Great 'casion hae we a' to weep,
An' cleed our skins in mourning deep,   *clothe*
For Gregory *death* will fairly keep
    To take his nap;
He'll till the resurrection sleep
    As sound's a tap.

Patricius Hamiltonus

Martyr Andreapoli xxviii. Feb. An. Christi, 1527

E caelo alluxit primam Germania lucem
    Qua Lanus, et vitreis qua fluit Albis aquis.
Intulit hinc lucem nostrae Dux praevius orae.
    O felix terra! hoc si foret usa duce!
Dira superstitio grassata tyrannide in omnes,
    Omniaque involvens Cimmeriis tenebris.
Illa nequit lucem hanc sufferre. Ergo omnis in unam,
    Fraude, odiis, furiis, turba cruenta coit.
Igne cremant. Vivus lucis qui fulserat igne,
    Par erat ut moriens lumina ab igne daret.

Patrick Hamilton

Martyred at St Andrews, 28 February 1527
translated by Robert Crawford from the Latin of John Johnston
(c.1568–1611)

The first light dawned out of a German heaven,
Where the Lahn flows, and the glass-clear Elbe.
We had a leader bringing us this light;
A happy Scotland would have let him lead,
But all were tyrannized by superstition,
All *in tenebris*, clogged with a thick murk
That hated brilliance. So, all against one,
With lies and anger they scapegoated him,
Burned him alive. A shining light in life,
In his death too he brought enlightenment.

A Poem in my Rucksack

One of the crucial decisions I made at this time was to spend my junior year abroad, at St Andrews in Scotland ...

I recall with pristine clarity that evening when I arrived in St Andrews on the train from Leuchars Junction (a railway link no longer in existence). I paced up and down the three main streets of the town, all of which converge at the ruined cathedral, and St Rule's Tower: a haunting outcrop of medieval architecture. I went down to the harbour below the cathedral, and walked out to the end of a stone pier, and sat looking across an expanse of black water, a sky filled with stars. The air was salty and cool, and I could hear the water crashing in the rocks. It was all so bracing and, curiously, familiar, even though I had never been to such a place before. St Andrews felt like home right from the beginning.

My taste for poetry and fiction deepened considerably during my junior year. There was an active intellectual culture in my residence hall, St Regs, and I listened eagerly to fellow students as they talked about Eliot and Yeats. I remember in particular a night when an older student came into my room and read, with a sonorous Scottish accent, 'The Love Song of J. Alfred Prufrock'. His reading of that poem, in a suitably dramatic voice, made more of an impression on me than any course I had ever taken in poetry, and to this day I regard reading aloud to my students from poetry and fiction as one of the essential things I do in the classroom. What I try to convey in these readings is *tone*, the attitude of the speaker in the text toward the material at hand. Over the years, a surprising number of students have told me that they learned to read closely by listening to me read aloud.

During my first term in St Andrews, I was fortunate to have a young tutor called Tony Ashe, whose seminars were occasions for alert, forceful confrontations with a wide range of texts, from Pope and Wordsworth to Eliot and Yeats. Tony introduced me to Gerard Manley Hopkins, a poet who seemed almost to reinvent the physical world with his language, in his journals as well as his poems, giving it freshness and tangibility. Tony treated each member of his seminar with a respectful diffidence, expecting students to say intelligent and serious things, and to discover ways that the text at hand embodied, or bodied forth, experience. He was working in the New Critical mode, having studied at St Andrews and Oxford during the fifties and early sixties, when Empson and Leavis were still in high fashion. In keeping with this tradition, he often stripped the poems of their historical/biographical contexts, much as I. A. Richards had done at Cambridge in the twenties. In retrospect, I see that my teaching life began there, around a highly polished oak table in Castle House, where the tall windows looked out over the icy North Sea and a huge, cobalt sky. I found myself being articulate in a classroom for the first time, discussing matters that felt dear and relevant to my intellectual and spiritual life. The intensity of this experience was transforming.

* * *

I returned to St Andrews in late September, eager to start on my graduate work – the B.Phil. thesis on Gerard Manley Hopkins. The chairman of the English Department – my supervisor – was called, simply and deferentially, The Professor. In those days, there was only one professor, the person who ran the department. This was true of every department: one professor per subject. Everyone else worked as his assistant. In the English Department, this included Tony Ashe. We all talked with a kind of bemused affection about The Professor, A. F. Falconer. He was a tiny, wizened man with long hair and a distracted manner. He looked a lot like Shakespeare in the famous etching: a thin face, a long nose, a high forehead. His baggy, pinstriped suits seemed to have been made for a man much taller and fatter, the sleeves coming down over his palms, the cuffs billowing over his shoes. He was a Shakespearean scholar of no great repute, the author of an eccentric book called *Shakespeare and the Sea*, in which he argued that during the lost years of the Bard's life he must have been an officer in the Royal Navy, otherwise he could not have known so much about the habits of seagoing types, such as

Othello. A wonderfully ambiguous blurb on the dust jacket suggests that this book should be 'put on every seagoing man's bookshelf, and kept there'. The Professor had followed up this tome with an even more bizarrely idiosyncratic study: *A Glossary of Gunnery and Naval Terms in Shakespeare.*

In truth, I liked old Falconer, and would frequently stop by for chats in his windy office in Castle House.

Although officially a student of Falconer's, I was in reality working with Tony Ashe, who guided me briskly and intelligently through my B.Phil. thesis on Hopkins and my Ph.D. thesis on Theodore Roethke. ...

Lunchtime at the Ashe house on North Street was always a rambling seminar, and various members of staff and friends – mostly graduate students like myself – brought bits and pieces to the meal: cans of tuna, loaves of bread, hunks of cheddar, packets of instant soup. For dessert, we had what we called 'chemical pudding' – a sweet, glutinous substance that came in various pastel shades. We talked, and joked, about everything – from literature and current events to history and the arts; I picked up an immense amount of historical and literary knowledge at those lunches. When literary visitors came through town to lecture or read, they would often join us for lunch, swelling the crowd, adding a dimension to the conversation. Among the poets who stomped through the blue front door at North Street were Alastair Reid, Seamus Heaney, Edwin Morgan, Stephen Spender, Iain Crichton Smith, Norman MacCaig, Philip Hobsbaum, and Anne Stevenson.

In St Andrews, I had a mentor and good friend in Alastair Reid, the Scottish poet and translator. I often cycled out to his cottage by the North Sea, bearing a rough draft of a poem in my rucksack. We would sit side by side in his kitchen at Pilmour Cottage, his stone house overlooking the Old Course, as he dissected my latest effort. He would 'correct' my poem, as he said. I sat quietly and watched the language transform before my eyes, the weak adverbs absorbed into stronger verbs, the superfluous or boring adjective erased, contained in a stronger noun. Alastair taught by showing: ostentation, once again. He might cross out a weak phrase and invent a better one. He might rearrange or cancel lines or whole stanzas, refusing to treat any language as sacred. He questioned diction, tone, turns of phrase. His ear was flawless, and I learned how to write in the musical phrase, how to listen to my own poem.

Alastair worked his way through various poems and poets with me. I still recall quite vividly an afternoon when I complained that I did not really understand Yeats's poem 'Among School Children'. He took me through the poem, stanza by stanza, giving me various possibilities for interpretation. It was stunning but modest as well, paying close attention to the words themselves. He showed me how the seemingly unrelated stanzas fit together, reinforced and reinterpreted the stanzas that went before. He read aloud that sonorous final stanza, and talked about the summary images: the tree, which cannot be separated into its various parts: leaf, blossom, bole. Or the dancer that becomes the dance, the creator so merged with the activity of making meaning that one cannot separate them. Poem and poet. Dance and dancer. The poem became an intimate part of my own psychology, and I look forward to teaching the poem at least once a year. When I do, I hear Alastair talking . . .

An Aura all its Own

When I go back to Scotland, I gravitate mostly to the East Neuk of Fife, that richly farmed promontory jutting into the North Sea to the north-east of Edinburgh, specifically to the town of St Andrews, a well-worn place that has persisted in my memory from the time I first went there, a very young student at a very ancient university. I have come and gone at intervals over some thirty years, and St Andrews has changed less in that time than any other place I can think of. It is a singular place, with an aura all its own. For a start, it has a setting unfailingly beautiful to behold in any weather – the curve of St Andrews Bay sweeping in from the estuary of the River Eden across the washed expanse of the West Sands, backed by the windy green of the golf courses, to the town itself, spired, castled, and cathedraled, punctuated by irregular bells, cloistered and grave, with grey stone roofed in slate or red tile, kempt ruins and a tidy harbour, the town backed by green and gold fields with their stands of ancient trees. If it has the air of a museum, that is no wonder, for it sits placidly on top of a horrendous past. From the twelfth century on, it was in effect the ecclesiastical capital of Scotland, but the Reformation spelled its downfall: its vast cathedral was sacked, and by the seventeen-hundreds the place had gone into a sad decline. Its history looms rather grimly, not just in the carefully tended ruins of castle and cathedral but in the well-walked streets; inset in the cobblestones at the entrance to St Salvator's College quadrangle are the initials 'P.H.', for Patrick Hamilton, who was burned as a martyr on that spot in 1528; students acquire the superstition of never treading on the initials. With such a weighty past so tangibly present, the townspeople assume the air and manner of custodians, making themselves as comfortable and inconspicuous as they can among the ruins, and turning up their noses at the transients – the students, the golfers, the summer visitors. Yet, as in all such situations, it is the transients who sustain the place, who flock into it, year in, year out, to the present-day shrines of the university and the golf courses.

The date of the founding of the University of St Andrews is given, variously, as 1411 or 1412: the ambiguity arises from the fact that in fifteenth-century Scotland the year began on March 25, and the group of scholars who founded the institution received their charter in February of that dubious year. Such matters are the stuff of serious controversy in St Andrews. As students, we felt admitted to a venerable presence, even if the curriculum appeared to have undergone only minimal alteration since 1411. A kind of wise mist enveloped the place, and it seemed that we could not help absorbing it, unwittingly. The professors lectured into space, in an academic trance; we took notes, or borrowed them; the year's work culminated in a series of written examinations on set texts, which a couple of weeks of intense immersion, combined with native cunning and a swift pen, could take care of. What that serious, gravid atmosphere did was to make the present shine, in contradistinction to the past. Tacitly and instinctively, we relished the place more than the dead did or could, and we felt something like an obligation to fly in the face of the doleful past. The green woods and the sea surrounded us, the library, and an ocean of time. When I left St Andrews to go into the Navy in the Second World War, the place, over my shoulder, took on a never-never aura – not simply the never-neverness of college years but as contrast to the troubled state of the times. It appeared to me, in that regard, somewhat unreal.

In its human dimension, St Andrews embodied the Scotland I chose to leave behind me. The spirit of Calvin, far from dead, stalked the countryside, ever present in a pinched wariness, a wringing of the hands. We were taught to expect the worst – miserable sinners, we could not expect more. A rueful doom ruffles the Scottish spirit. It takes various spoken forms. That summer, a man in Edinburgh said to me, 'See you tomorrow, if we're spared,' bringing me to a horrified standstill. 'Could be worse' is a regular verbal accolade; and that impassioned cry from the Scottish spirit 'It's no' right!' declares drastically that *nothing* is right, nothing will ever be right – a cry of doom. Once at an international rugby match between Scotland and England in which the Scots, expected to win comfortably, doggedly snatched defeat from the jaws of victory, a friend of mine noticed two fans unroll a carefully prepared hand-stitched banner bearing the legend 'WE WUZ ROBBED'. The wariness is deep-rooted. I prize the encounter I once had with a local woman on the edge of St Andrews, on a heady spring day. I exclaimed my pleasure in the day, at which she darkened and muttered, 'We'll pay for it, we'll pay for it' – a poem in itself.

> It was a day peculiar to this piece of the planet,
> when larks rose on long thin strings of singing
> and the air shifted with the shimmer of actual angels.
> Greenness entered the body. The grasses
> shivered with presences, and sunlight
> stayed like a halo on hair and heather and hills.
> Walking into town, I saw, in a radiant raincoat,
> the woman from the fish-shop. 'What a day it is!'
> cried I, like a sunstruck madman.
> And what did she have to say for it?
> Her brow grew bleak, her ancestors raged in their graves
> as she spoke with their ancient misery:
> 'We'll pay for it, we'll pay for it, we'll pay for it!'

* * *

St Andrews turned out to be my point of departure. I left it after a brief first year to go into the Navy, and by the time I got back, after the end of the Second World War, I had seen the Mediterranean, the Red Sea, the Indian Ocean, and enough ports of call, enough human variety, to make St Andrews seem small and querulous. Yet the allure still hung over it, and I felt it still – felt the place to be, especially in the wake of the war years, something of an oasis. I have come and gone countless times since, returning, perhaps, because its citizens can be relied on to maintain it in as much the same order as is humanly possible. (In every town in

Scotland, you will find houses occupied by near-invisible people whose sole function seems to be to maintain the house and garden in immaculate condition, as unobtrusively as they can. In New Galloway once, I watched a woman scrubbing the public sidewalk in front of her house with soap and water on two occasions during the day. She may have done it oftener, but I did not feel like extending my vigil.) The presence of the university and the golfing shrines has allowed St Andrews to preserve a kind of feudal structure: the university, being residential, houses and feeds its students, administers and staffs itself, and so provides a pyramid of work for the town, as does golf, whose faithful pilgrims keep hotels, caddies, and sellers of repainted golf balls in business. Others retire there, to its Peter Pan-like permanence, bringing their savings with them. As a result, the place has a bookish, well-to-do air, a kind of leisured aloofness this side of smug. I liked to imagine the wide cobbled centre of Market Street set with tables with red-checked tablecloths, between the Star Hotel and the Cross Keys, crisscrossed with singing waiters – Italians or, better, Brazilians, carrying laden trays, sambaing, animating the place, rescuing it from its prim residents, forever hurrying home close to the old stone walls, eyes down, like nuns.

> I do not think of the academy
> in the whirl of days. It does not change. I do.
> The place hangs in my past like an engraving.
> I went back once to lay a wreath on it,
> and met discarded selves I scarcely knew.
>
> It has a lingering aura, leather bindings,
> a smell of varnish and formaldehyde,
> a certain dusty holiness in the cloisters.
> We used to race our horses on the sand
> away from it, manes flying, breathing hard.

Trailing to the library of an afternoon,
we saw the ivy crawling underneath
the labyrinthine bars on the window ledges.
I remember the thin librarian's look of hate
as we left book holes in her shelves, like missing teeth.

On evenings doomed by bells, we felt the sea
creep up, we heard the temperamental gulls
wheeling in clouds about the kneeworn chapel.
They keened on the knifing wind like student souls.
Yet we would dent the stones with our own footfalls.

Students still populate the place, bright starlings,
their notebooks filled with scribbled parrot-answers
to questions they unravel every evening
in lamplit pools of spreading argument.
They slash the air with theory, like fencers.

Where is the small, damp-browed professor now?
Students have pushed him out to sea in a boat
of lecture-notes. Look, he bursts into flame!
How glorious a going for one whose words
had never struck a spark on the whale-road.

And you will find retainers at their posts,
wearing their suits of age, brass buttons, flannel,
patrolling lawns they crop with careful scissors.
They still will be in silver-haired attendance
to draw lines through our entries in the annals.

It is illusion, the academy.
In truth, the ideal talking-place to die.
Only the landscape keeps a sense of growing.
The towers are floating on a shifting sea.
You did not tell the truth there, nor did I.

Think of the process – moments becoming poems
which stiffen into books in the library,
and later, lectures, books about the books,
footnotes and dates, a stone obituary.
Do you wonder that I shun the academy?

It anticipates my dying, turns to stone
too quickly for my taste. It is a language
nobody speaks, refined to ritual:
the precise writing on the blackboard wall,
the drone of requiem in the lecture hall.

I do not think much of the academy
in the drift of days. It does not change. I do.
This poem will occupy the library
but I will not. I have not done with doing.
I did not know the truth there, nor did you.

Back on the Beach

Ah, yes, the summer of love. I spent it, along with most other summers in the 1960s, at Kinkell Braes caravan park in St Andrews. I think we first went there in 1964, and that was us every holiday until around 1970. In 1964, I was four years old, so a caravan suited me. That first year, I managed to tear the labels off every can of food in the cupboard, leading to a fortnight of adventurous meals. But the holiday really started the moment the car arrived in our cul-de-sac back in Bowhill, at that time still a mining village. Our SSHA housing scheme had been built in 1961, and most of the families had moved *en masse* from the prefabs where I'd been born.

The car would belong to a family friend or relative (neither of my parents could drive). We'd start loading it for the journey, and all the neighbours would come out to watch, some of them pressing last-minute gifts of sweets or pocket money into my hand. They'd stay to see us off – mum, dad, my big sister, me and the driver – as though some great expedition were being undertaken. I'd have my knees up around my chin, feet resting on a bag filled with picnic stuff or a brand new beachball, bound for a distant region (nearly 30 miles by road) where the word 'links' didn't immediately connote sausages.

The Fife holiday coincided with the Glasgow Fair Fortnight. I was never sure if 'fair' referred to some West Coast festival or to the weather. Our neighbours at the caravan site were a mix of familiar faces from back home and Glaswegians boasting funny accents and Rangers and Celtic strips. Ironically, my main memory of the 'fair' fortnight is of rain, leading to stir-crazy times. Was it hell on my parents? I can't remember; certainly I have no memory of arguments, just long games of Newmarket, played for matches as the latest downpour hammered on the roof. Even now I'm not sure whether I won fairly and squarely, or whether an adult conspiracy was afoot. Ditto the putting green, where I won more than my fair share of rounds. At night there'd be sputtering gas mantles and the smell of mothballs as our mum got the beds ready. There was something magical about the way the bench seats suddenly became our sleeping quarters, but it was no place for the claustrophobic.

The caravan, rented from some acquaintance back home, didn't have a toilet or running water, so there were constant trips to the amenities block and the standpipe. At night, with the lights on, the block attracted jenny-long-legs, and I could barely be persuaded to step inside to use the toilet or brush my teeth. I don't recall any baths or showers, which might explain why we came to take so many dips in the chilly North Sea.

Even aged five or six, I think I knew that my parents had to be careful with money. They scrimped and saved all year to ensure we had a proper fortnight's holiday. My dad worked in a grocer's shop in Lochgelly; my mum prepared meals in a school dinner kitchen. Dad had a fund of funny stories about working in the shop (and, it seemed, about everything else, from boyhood mishaps to army service), and could be relied on to tell them again and again if the weather stayed damp.

But when the sun broke through, we'd be off towards town, which meant walking down the steep scary brae: a deep hole one side of the path, cliff face the other. When I revisited Kinkell Braes recently – my first trip back since childhood – I made straight for the scary brae. It didn't seem to have changed. Moles had been busy the length of the path, and a sick-looking hare sat off to one side. The cliffs have been fenced off, and now sport a warning sign. To my amazement, the scary hole is still there, too – or at least, something approximating it. Like the cliffs, it's been fenced off and doesn't seem quite the same. Maybe my memory has played tricks on me, or maybe it's just not the same hole. But it's there, in about the right place. I was terrified of it, would lie sleepless at night worrying about falling in. When we walked down that path, I shuffled past it sideways. On the run-up to each summer holiday I'd have nightmares about it. Now ... well, it's just a hole in the ground, a water conduit from the caravan site. I stood there for quite some time this trip, daring it to frighten me, trying to summon back some of the power it had once held. To no effect.

Once past the scary hole, you're at sea level, the beach spread out, stretching out to the harbour with the town's rooftops in the distance. We would make for the beach with deckchairs and towels, or head for the putting green. The putting green is still there, or at least its undulations remain, fenced off from the path on one side and the tributary on the other. There was an anonymous kiosk next to it, firmly closed for the winter, giving no clues as to whether putting could still be played, weather permitting.

I was spending a few days in St Andrews, ostensibly giving talks and a lecture and doing some research for my next book. But really I was wallowing in the past. So much of John Rebus's past is my own that when I decided he needed to visit St Andrews, I decided he'd spent caravan holidays there as a child. I wanted him to see the place through my eyes, the wanderer returned. When we moved back to Scotland in 1996, I'd taken my wife on a drive through the East Neuk. Part of me wanted to settle back in Fife. I couldn't see Miranda rubbing her hands in glee at the thought of a semi in Cardenden or Lochore, but thought the likes of St Monans or Pittenweem might do the trick. It was November, cold and dark, the streets empty. I think Miranda said something like: 'Bit of a long way from anywhere.'

Which seemed true, even when I was a kid. Even now, driving north from Edinburgh, leaving the M90 at Junction 8, there's over 20 miles of A and B roads before one reaches St Andrews. The place has a Brigadoon quality to it: suddenly it's there in front of you, seemingly untouched by time. But time has certainly moved on. When I was deciding, aged 17, which university I would grace with my presence, St Andrews got checked out early on. I attended the open day, my head full of American writers – Heller, Bellow, Kesey – and asked someone from the English Department what modern writers they studied. 'Oh,' he said airily, 'we stretch as far as Milton.' Nowadays, the university boasts such heady delights as Scottish Literature and – whisper it – creative writing, and staff of the calibre of Robert Crawford and Douglas Dunn, both well-known creative writers themselves. It's sussed in other ways, too. Heading down an alley, I came across a Schools Liaison Office and an American Enrolment Office.

When the Rankin family headed from the harbour into town, we'd walk past the university buildings. There were precious few students around in July, so I had to ask my dad what the various signs meant. 'Department of Logic and Metaphysics, dad. What's that?' He probably made something up. Most certainly I believed him.

There's new housing along the seashore now, and an indoor swimming pool, but the beach still looks ready for a bit of excavation work with a bucket and spade. My sister and I had a favourite game of drawing the outline of a speedboat in the damp sand, then sitting inside it, pretending we were skimming across the waves. Out at sea, a real boat or two would always seem to be at anchor. Our dad said they were Russian spy ships and that the frequent low-flying jets had been scrambled from Leuchars to keep an eye on them. It couldn't be that every summer was cold in the Sixties (otherwise how to explain my memories of a peeling back and neck?), but all the holiday snaps I've got seem cold. They might be in black and white, but curiously you can tell that my sister Linda and I are blue with cold as we huddle in our swimsuits under thin bath towels.

Thankfully, there was more to do in St Andrews than visit the caravan site shop or risk hypothermia on the beach. For one thing, there was St Rule's Tower, which was said to be haunted. From the top there was – and remains – a spectacular view of the town, sea and countryside. Though this time round, it being December, the only other people in the vicinity were workmen doing something to the stonework of one of the walls. At one point, they seemed to vanish, but all they'd done was leap an exterior wall as a short-cut to their van.

Haunted or not, St Andrews was just the place to fire a young boy's already active imagination. One of my favourite spots was the Castle's bottle dungeon, a gloomy cave of a place with just the one entrance and source of light – the neck of the bottle-shaped cell. Prisoners would be dropped into the dungeon from above, falling 20-odd feet into what would be their final, unwelcome home. Between this, the scary hole, and the ghosts that could fling you at any moment from the top of St Rule's Tower, is it any wonder I grew up with a fear of heights?

This trip, I didn't visit the Castle. It was late on in the day when I arrived, and the entry fee looked a bit steep (that fear of heights again). Instead, I walked on towards the Old Course. They used to post the round fees on a sign next to the club house. This was back in the days when St Andrews only seemed to have the two courses – Old and New. (These days it boasts no fewer than six.) I remember how expensive we thought it was, certainly compared to our putting green at the East Sands, but then none of us were golfers. These days there's no sign of how much a round will cost you, but the area around the club house has certainly changed. For a start, there's the British Golf Museum, which seemed busy even on a dreich winter's afternoon. Then there's the Sea Life Centre, new-looking yet also scuffed and somewhat tired, and across from it something going by the name of Crumbs Pavilion Tea Room, a structure which must have been there in the Sixties, though I don't remember it. I was pleased to see that the Woollen Mill had not, however, changed location. I don't recall enjoying my visits to it as a child. No boy my age liked clothes shops.

I much preferred the toy shop in the town centre. I bought a bright red pogo stick there, against my parents' wishes. Their argument was that it wouldn't fit in the car, but I think they also knew it would be a waste of money. I got my way though, and of course found that I couldn't master the stupid thing. It seemed to have no sense of balance. The only person I ever remember using it was my eldest sister's husband, who worked at Leuchars, servicing all those low-flying jets. He bounced it around the paved area of our back garden for a while until the rubber foot split. He was good at that sort of thing. Once, he went into our attic for some reason and put his foot through my bedroom ceiling.

A much more successful buy than the pogo stick was my first ever vinyl record. It was a 45rpm release with a picture cover. The picture was of Action Man. Side one purported to be my favourite doll's theme song ('Action Man is here/Action Man is here/On land, at sea and in the air/In action everywhere'). Side two was made up of battle sound effects, complete with air strikes. You were supposed to play this while putting Action Man through his paces, though with a running time of under three minutes, it was more Desert Storm than World War II. I've never met anyone else who owned that record, and quite a few who've doubted its existence. The year after I bought it, my Action Man tragically died under interrogation. But that didn't matter: I'd bought a record. And in the summer of 1972, at Butlin's in Ayr, I'd start on the road towards bankruptcy proper by buying *School's Out* and *Silver Machine*.

Walking down Market Street after all these years, I was stunned to find myself placing the toy shop, the one where I'd bought the pogo stick and the Action Man record. I saw a turret, saw a spot where the road widened ... and knew exactly where the shop sat. It's not a toy shop now though. It's an ice cream parlour, which pleased me so much I wandered in and ordered a cone. The centre of St Andrews has resolutely failed to embrace the usual fast-food chains and shoe outlets which plague most Scottish towns. Perhaps this is because it can afford not to. An air of inviolable prosperity hangs over the place, as well as a certain schizophrenia: holiday destination for the caravan classes as well as for three-handicap Japanese golfers. Ancient seat of learning, but also a place where a severed hand can turn up in a post-box.

My mother died when I was 19, my father ten years later. In returning to St Andrews, I think I was hoping to relive a portion of my life with them, to stir up happy memories. It certainly worked. The putting green and toy shop ... I probably hadn't thought of these places in a couple of decades. So many sites brought back a memory of some situation, or something my mum or dad had said. Staring at what had been the putting green, I saw my father bent over his putter, flicking the ball so it travelled along the curve of a hillock. I saw my mother send the ball towards Kinness Burn, me pelting after it in chase, arms flapping like wings. Turning to face the shore, I saw sand castles and tunnels, saw me burying the feet of my mother as she slept in her deckchair. I saw us waving at the ships on the horizon, just in case they were studying us, to let them know we knew.

I don't visit Fife often these days. There's not much left there in the way of family, not much to take me back to Cardenden. The last time I went back, stopping the car at the end of our cul-de-sac, I felt a stab of sadness. Where we'd had a small, neat garden, with a lawn my father mowed so we could practise our putting, now there was a driveway with a car. Almost all our original neighbours were gone. It reminded me of the title of Allan Massie's first novel: *Change and Decay in All Around I See*. St Andrews did much to remedy that.

I headed back towards Kinkell Braes. The sick hare was no longer to be seen. Maybe it had fallen down the scary hole. The caravans all seemed bigger and posher than the one we'd stayed in, and the amenities were better, too. But the shop was still there, the shop where I'd gone to buy comics and the family's *Sunday Post*, turning to the Merry Mac Fun Page so I could do my favourite picture puzzle. The puzzle they called a 'rebus'.

SAMUEL JOHNSON

Eminently Adapted

Saint Andrews seems to be a place eminently adapted to study and education, being situated in a populous, yet a cheap country, and exposing the minds and manners of young men neither to the levity and dissoluteness of a capital city, nor to the gross luxury of a town of commerce, places naturally unpropitious to learning; in one the desire of knowledge easily gives way to the love of pleasure, and in the other, is in danger of yielding to the love of money.

JAMES BOSWELL

I Happened to Ask

After what Dr Johnson has said of St Andrews, which he had long wished to see, as our oldest university, and the seat of our Primate in the days of episcopacy, I can say little. Since the publication of Dr Johnson's book, I find that he has been censured for not seeing here the ancient chapel of *St Rule*, a curious piece of sacred architecture. But this was neither his fault nor mine. We were both of us abundantly desirous of surveying such sort of antiquities: but neither of us knew of this. I am afraid the censure must fall on those who did not tell us of it. In every place, where there is any thing worth of observation, there should be a short printed directory for strangers, such as we find in all the towns of Italy, and in some of the towns in England. I was told that there is a manuscript account of St Andrews, by Martin, secretary to Archbishop Sharp; and that one Douglas has published a small account of it. I inquired at a bookseller's but could not get it. Dr Johnson's veneration for the Hierarchy is well known. There is no wonder then, that he was affected with a strong indignation, while he beheld the ruins of religious magnificence. I happened to ask where John Knox was buried. Dr Johnson burst out, 'I hope in the high-way. I have been looking at his reformations.'

ROBERT FERGUSSON

To the Principal and Professors of the University of St Andrews, on their Superb Treat to Dr Samuel Johnson

St Andrews town may look right gawsy,	*handsome*
Nae grass will grow upon her cawsey,	*pavement*
Nor wa'-flowers of a yellow dye,	
Glour dowy o'er her ruins high,	*sadly*
Sin Samy's head weel pang'd wi' lear,	*crammed; learning*
Has seen the *Alma Mater* there:	
Regents, my winsome billy boys!	*Professors; good lads*
'Bout him you've made an unco noise;	
Nae doubt for him your bells wad clink	
To find him upon Eden's brink,	
An' a' things nicely set in order,	
Wad kep him on the Fifan border:	
I'se warrant now frae France an' Spain,	*[of Fife]*
Baith cooks and scullions mony ane	
Wad gar the pats an' kettles tingle	
Around the college kitchen ingle,	*fire*

To fleg frae a' your craigs the roup,	*drive; throats; hoarseness*
Wi' reeking het and crieshy soup;	*hot; greasy*
And snails and puddocks mony hunder	*frogs; hundred*
Wad beeking lie the hearth-stane under,	*baking*
Wi' roast and boild, an' a' kin kind,	
To heat the body, cool the mind.	
But hear me lads! gin I'd been there,	*if*
How I wad trimm'd the bill o' fare!	
For ne'er sic surly wight as he	*man*
Had met wi' sic respect frae me.	
Mind ye what Sam, the lying loun!	*fellow*
Has in his Dictionar laid down?	
That aits in England are a feast	*oats*
To cow an' horse, an' sican beast,	
While in Scots ground this growth was common	
To gust the gab o' man and woman.	*please; mouth*
Tak tent, ye Regents! then, an' hear	*pay attention*
My list o' gudely hamel gear,	*homely food*
Sic as ha'e often rax'd the wyme	*stretched; stomach*
O' blyther fallows many time;	
Mair hardy, souple, steive an' swank,	*sturdy; smart*
Than ever stood on Samy's shank.	
Imprimis, then, a haggis fat,	*Firstly*
Weel tottled in a seything pat,	*simmered; pot*
Wi' spice and ingans well ca'd thro',	*onions*
Had help'd to gust the stirrah's mow,	*rude man's mouth*
And plac'd itsel in truncher clean	
Before the gilpy's glowrin een.	*man's; eyes*
Secundo, then a gude sheep's head	
Whase hide was singit, never flead,	*flayed*
And four black trotters cled wi' girsle,	*gristle*

Bedown his throat had learn'd to hirsle.   glide
What think ye neist, o' gude fat brose   *next; [dish of oatmeal]*
To clag his ribs? a dainty dose!
And white and bloody puddins routh,
To gar the Doctor skirl, O Drouth!   *make; scream*
Whan he cou'd never houp to merit
A cordial o' reaming claret,
But thraw his nose, and brize and pegh   *puff*
O'er the contents o' sma' ale quegh: *quaich*
Then let his wisdom girn and snarl
O'er a weel-tostit girdle farl,   *cake*
An' learn, that maugre o' his wame,   *despite; belly*
Ill bairns are ay best heard at hame.

      Drummond, lang syne, o' Hawthornden,
The wyliest an' best o' men,
Has gi'en you dishes ane or mae,
That wad ha' gard his grinders play,
Not to *roast beef*, old England's life,
But to the auld *east nook of Fife*,
Where Creilian crafts cou'd weel ha'e gi'en   *[of Crail]*
Scate-rumples to ha'e clear'd his een: *skate-tails*
Than neist whan Samy's heart was faintin,
He'd lang'd for scate to mak him wanton.

      Ah! willawins, for Scotland now,   *wellaway*
Whan she maun stap ilk birky's mow   *man's mouth*
Wi' eistacks, grown as 'tware in pet   *dainties, freakish heat*
In foreign land, or green-house het,
When cog o' brose an' cutty spoon   *bowl; short-handled*
Is a' our cottar childer's boon,
Wha thro' the week, till Sunday's speal,   *rest*
Toil for pease-clods an' gude lang kail.   *pease-loaf; cabbage*

Devall then, Sirs, and never send   *leave off*
For daintiths to regale a friend,   *dainties*
Or, like a torch at baith ends burning,
Your house 'll soon grow mirk and mourning.
      What's this I hear some cynic say?
Robin, ye loun! its nae fair play;
Is there nae ither subject rife
To clap your thumb upon but Fife?
Gi'e o'er, young man, you'll meet your corning,
Than caption war, or charge o' horning;
Some canker'd surly sour-mow'd carline   *old woman*
Bred near the abbey o' Dumfarline,
Your shoulders yet may gi'e a lounder,   *blow*
An' be of verse the mal-confounder.
      Come on, ye blades! but 'ere ye tulzie,   *quarrel*
Or hack our flesh wi' sword or gulzie,   *knife*
Ne'er shaw your teeth, nor look like stink,
Nor o'er an empty bicker blink: *beaker*
What weets the wizen an' the wyme,   *throat; stomach*
Will mend your prose and heal my rhyme.

Lines Written Under the Portrait of Robert Fergusson, the Poet

Curse on ungrateful man, that can be pleas'd,
And yet can starve the author of the pleasure.
O thou my elder brother in misfortune,
By far my elder brother in the muse,
With tears I pity thy unhappy fate!
Why is the bard unpitied by the world,
Yet has so keen a relish of its pleasures?

Robert Fergusson Night
St Andrews University A.D. 2000

All the Fergussons are black
I've heard said in the Outback.
Sub rosa, the Scots empire ranged wide.
I hope Scotland proportions her pride
now to the faith her lads kept with
all the subject folks they slept with.
I know for you this wasn't an issue.
Madness made a white man of you

disastrously young. You stayed alive
just long enough to revive
from Scottish models and kings
such mediaeval things
as documentary verse-television
and writing in Scots for the brain.
In that, you set the great precedent
for every vernacular and variant

the world-reach of English would present.
Now you're two hundred and fifty
and gin some power the giftie
gied ye of a writer-in-revenance
you'd find a death-cult called Romance
both selling and preserving a scrubbed Reekie
and the now-posh Highlands. Very freaky.
You might outdo Dr Johnson in polite

St Andrews now, that Reformation bombsite.
I fear you mightn't outdraw golf there:
golf keeps from the door the wolf there –
but nobody does what you showed aversion
to already in your time, poetical inversion.
Metrics too, now, are Triassic pent amateur
and 'Rhyme is for Negroes', I heard in Berlin:
the speaker was a literary Finn.

Such talk, now at last, is a sin
in place of much that wasn't. Madness
for instance. The Bedlams yielded to medicine:
even madness has, a little. Madness:
would you rise from the grave back through madness?
It took you and left us Burns
of Burns Night. Many jubilant returns:
this at last is Robert Fergusson Night.

DON PATERSON

Horseman

efter Rilke, i.m. Rab Fergusson

Look up at the skeh: whar's the constellation
crehd 'The Horseman'? Gi'en this is wir sang –
a baist's wull, and some heh'r distillation
that ca's and brakes it, and wham it kerts alang.

Is this no' jist wir sinneny existence,
gaddin wirsels on, reinin wirsels back in?
Road an sheddin; then ae tip – a new distance
fa's awa, and the twa are yin again.

But this is a' wrang, surely? Dinna they signifeh
jist the rake wih tak thegither? As it is,
thir sindered beh the table and the trough.

Even thir starnie union is a leh;
a' wih can dae is doorly insist
wih merk it up there. Mibbe thon's enough.

crehd – called; *ca* – drive; *kert* – carry; *sinneny* – sinewy; *gaddin* – goading;
sheddin – fork, parting; *tip* – touch; *rake* – wander; *starnie* – starry

WALTER SCOTT

Solemn Vows to Pay

from *Marmion, Canto First*

'But I have solemn vows to pay,
And may not linger by the way,
    To fair St Andrews bound,
Within the ocean-cave to pray,
Where good Saint Rule his holy lay,
From midnight to the dawn of day,
    Sung to the billows' sound.'

from *Papistry Storm'd*

I sing the steir, strabush, and strife,   *stir; tumult*
Whan, bickerin' frae the towns o' Fife,
Great bangs of bodies, thick and rife,   *crowds*
    Gaed to Sanct Androis town,
And, wi' John Calvin i' their heads,
And hammers i' their hands and spades,
Enrag'd at idols, mass, and beads,
    Dang the Cathedral down ...   *smashed*

* * *

As they cam' to the Prior-muir,
And saw Sanct Androis town and towr
    Atween them and the sea,
A wee they haltit to look down
Upon the multi-towred town,
That on her mountain o' renown
    Sat in her majestie;
Her sindry steeples, shootin' high,
Amid the schimmer o' the sky,
They set themsels, wi' curious eye,
    To reckon up and tell:
Her goodlie, great cathedral, spread
Upon the mountain's lordlie head,
In leviathan length, becrown'd
I' the middle, and at ilka bound,
Wi towr and spindyl turrets round,
    They mark'd and noted well ...

* * *

'Sae whair thy altars glister now,
Shall craps o' gosky dockens grow,   *crops; coarse*

And jag-arm'd nettles soon, I know,
The passer-by shall sting;
And schule-bairns, on a future day,
Shall be rampagin' in their play
Whare ance thy priests, in lang array,
Their matin-sangs did sing!'

DAVID LYNDSAY

Cardinal Beaton

from *The Tragedie, Of The Umquhyle Maist Reuerend Father Dauid Be
The Mercy Of God, Cardinall, And Archibyschope Of Sanctandrous.*

To the peple wes maid ane Spectakle
Off my dede and deformit Carioun.
Sum said it wes ane manifest Myrakle;
Sum said it was Diuine Punitioun,
So to be slane, in to my strang Dungeoun.
Quhen euery man had Iugit as hym lyste,   *judged as he saw fit*
Thay Saltit me, syne cloist me in an kyste.   *salted; then closed;*
chest

I laye vnburyit sewin monethtis and more,   *seven months*
Or I was borne to closter, kirk, or queir,   *Before*
In ane mydding, quhilk paine bene tyll deplore,   *midden*
Without suffrage of Chanoun, Monk, or freir.
All proude Prelatis at me may Lessonis leir,
Quhilk rang so lang, and so tryumphantlie,   *Who reigned*
Syne, in the dust, doung doun so dulefullie.   *crashed*

52

Diary Entries about John Knox

1571

Bot of all the benefites I haid that yeir was the coming of that maist notable profet and apostle of our nation, Mr Jhone Knox, to St Androis; wha, be the faction of the Quein occupeing the castell and town of Edinbruche, was compellit to remove thairfra with a number of the best, and chusit to com to St Androis. I hard him teatche ther the prophecie of Daniel that simmer, and the wintar following. I haid my pen and my litle book, and tuk away sic things as I could comprehend. In the opening upe of his text he was moderat the space of an halff houre; bot when he enterit to application, he maid me to grew and tremble, that I could nocht hald a pen to wryt. ... Mr Knox wald sum tymes com in and repose him in our Collage yeard, and call us schollars unto him and bless us, and exhort us to knaw God and his wark in our contrey, and stand be the guid cause, to use our tyme weill, and lern the guid instructiones, and follow the guid exemple of our maisters.

1574

Mr Knox ... being in St Androis he was very weak. I saw him everie day of his doctrine go hulie and fear, with a furring of martriks [*pine-marten fur*]about his neck, a staff in the an hand, and guid godlie Richart Ballanden, his servand, halding upe the uther oxtar, from the Abbay to the paroche kirk; and be the said Richart and another servant, lifted upe to the pulpit, whar he behovit to lean at his first entrie; bot or he haid done with his sermont, he was sae active and vigorus that he was lyk to ding that pulpit in blads [*i.e., to smash the pulpit*], and fly out of it!

Under

The man at the corner table is like a piece of water. He seems loose in the air, a kept river, a suspended lake. Somehow he has been drowned by life. The girl working in the hotel watches him as she moves around the room, between the other customers sitting in chairs or on stools alongside the raised counter. She looks at him while she is bending and lifting, refilling vessels and emptying catch trays. He seems like nothing within his clothing, occasionally his hand trickles out towards his glass and he lifts it and drinks slowly. If asked she couldn't describe his face well to anyone. It washes about in the air, sluicing over the features and making them indistinct. His hair might be dark or light, but each time she thinks she has it in focus it begins to eddy and reform. Even sitting close to the bar room fire in the back of the hotel doesn't dry him out into a distinctive human being. He remains soluble and quite without character. He sits in the darkest part of the bar, always at the same table. He seems to prefer it there. The girl watches him from different angles, searching for a solid anatomy, a body below the surface that could be touched, like divining in reverse, but the water remains close to him. She keeps a cloth in her hand when she is near him, ever ready to mop him up if he spills outwards and downwards, all over the floor.

She might be the only one who notices the man, people in the bar seem to pass through him, he'll disperse to allow their passage and then rebuild his dripping form. He isn't handsome, he isn't memorable. She can never really remember serving him or what he drinks. It feels as if they have never spoken, and yet he is familiar somehow. She doesn't know his name or what led him to this unusual condition, she keeps thinking one day she will speak to him and then she never does. But she watches him, rippling in the corner, and in a way he is compelling, because he hardly exists at all, because of his curious state, and he is beautiful for the soft shining liquid he is dressed in. Perhaps to everyone else he seems like a normal individual, not tall, not short, not too determined or too dangerous, and this is why he is paid no attention. Or perhaps he is just a figment of her imagination. She has trouble with herself in this place. She suffers from not knowing who she really is or why she's here, and has suspicions that doing this job isn't really for her, it is an error of some kind. She suffers from headaches and forgetfulness. The headaches are by far the worst. Every day brings another dull migraine which begins as a gathering of pain on the left side of her head, and gradually it increases, spreading across her skull, getting into her brain and behind her eyes, interfering with her vision and making her nauseous. The bright bay windows at the front of the hotel trouble her pupils, they let glaring light stream in, raw against her retinas. She tries to stay in the back of the bar, where it is dimmer and kinder to her tender head, and where the strange man comes and sits every day. By the end of her shift sometimes the discomfort is so bad that she is hallucinating mildly, seeing spots of light opening on the periphery like starkly lit exits out of dark tunnels. In her pocket she always keeps a few little pink pills, painkillers, but taking them seems not to make a difference and they taste chalky, brittle, like empty cartridges of calcium.

She blames herself for not being able to see the man at the corner table properly, she blames the sickness. Her distorted perspective ruins him, disrupts his atoms, dissolves his limbs and his identity. She can't shake that perpetual feeling of delirium and haze. Headaches aside, she is always busy and she works hard, there seems little else to do. The job is repetitive and continuous, it requires little variation, it numbs the soul as well as any pill. There are bottles to empty and fill. Surfaces to clear, pipes to clean. Food to prepare, drinks to serve. And people to steward. It's automatic, predictable, and it feels like time is repeating, replaying. Shift after shift after shift after shift. She sleeps upstairs, lives and works at the same hotel, and so there is never much change in her routine. At the end of the day she goes upstairs, her head wrought with pain, she lies down and falls asleep. The next day she wakes, gets up and comes down to begin another day. And so it goes on.

All the bar staff live in the hotel, it is a stipulation of the job, a benefit or a drawback she can't be sure which, and there are no other guests. They all say they feel the same way the girl does. They say they feel stuck here, doing the same thing again and again, over and over, wasting away, waiting for something better, something other – a version of life that makes sense and feels right, a version that is not so deadening. They say they feel unreal, dislocated. And that the place in which they reside and toil is washed over with an uncommon sense of stasis, its atmosphere is like anaesthetic. They are never roused enough to leave. They feel trapped, obliged to stay for reasons they do not understand, somehow not complicit in their lives, and barely able to remember their own names. All of them are inert, ill at ease and ill in their bodies much of the time. The girl notices that like her the rest of the staff also seem to nurse ailments and worry about their health; one of them limps badly and increasingly through the day, one has a thirst that can't be quenched, one has a heart murmur but can never find a pulse, one coughs ceaselessly and complains that it is too smoky. When they talk about this unhappiness during those quieter moments in the bar the conversation always brings alarm and upset and so they rarely do talk, instead they compulsively go about their work and their management of the bar; washing, pouring, cleaning, tending. It is wiser not to dwell on such things, they all agree. Otherwise they might begin to think they had taken a wrong turn somewhere in life. It would be an unbearable realization, mournful, funerary in a way.

The girl can't seem to turn her attention towards herself or these ideas, can't think of herself like that, she hasn't the determination or the energy. The best she can do is wonder about the predicament of others, their quiet anxiety, their non-being, like the man made of water. There are times his face does appear, usually at moments when the girl is least expecting it. She'll be doing the rounds, collecting glasses and squinting from the ache along her forehead, then for a brief moment the pain will lift and she'll look up. He will seem to solidify instantly at his table. The fluid against his face will rush away and she'll catch sight of what he really looks like. Or perhaps it's not what he looks like, because he seems revolving, ugly, something from a bad dream. He appears to be covered with worms and burying slugs, and underneath his skin is a sick rotten yellow like bruised fruit, and his eyes are monstrous, jellied and leaking over his cheeks like the lining inside a sea-snail's shell. Maybe it's only another trick of her eyes, she can't be sure. But at these times of disclosure she feels compelled more than ever to go towards him and say something, perhaps ask him to leave, perhaps just to lay a hand on him, finally, in comfort. Then the pain waxes and he is suddenly submerged by water again, lost, irrelevant. Whoever he is ceases to be. During these moments of clarity he reminds her of something, a picture she might have seen, a nightmare she may have had, something disturbing of the past which has stayed with her, lodged in her subconscious, like a pebble in the sole of a shoe. And because of this she feels responsible for him somehow, compelled to watch over him while on duty, like his keeper.

It occurs to her some days that this man is not so very different from the rest of the customers, that he is just a percentage in a meaningful element which makes up the surroundings. Working in this place is only ever a question of organizing liquid. Putting it into glasses, arranging a variety of it in bottles, tipping it out, tipping it into, flushing it away, rinsing things clean with it, managing the bodies it stays within, cleaning the stained receptacles where it is wasted at the end of her shift. Here in the hotel bar, there seems to be the constant threat of being subsumed by fluid, drenched by its onslaught, undone by its wet rub. And there are times, like towards the end of the day when her migraine is at its strongest, her eyesight faltering, that the whole place seems to be underwater and the customers move with inhibition on the ocean floor, turgid and sallow, swaying like weeds in the benthic winds. At these moments just moving across the room feels strenuous, nearly impossible, the girl is prohibited by space itself, and in addition to headaches she often has difficulty breathing. Sometimes the air feels too thick and silty for her lungs to use, or she's lacking the appropriate gills to filter it. Algae clouds and swarms in the air like dust. She find herself gasping for breath, breathing shallowly, desperate for oxygen, thinking she must kick upwards and break the surface soon, soon. She swims weakly from table to table, her arms gliding out like eels to recover pieces of bitten food. The weight of objects in the bar intensifies, becomes immovable, or a bag of coffee suddenly feels like nothing at all, like air. There are no terrestrial rules, no certain physical arrangements, there is no gravity, nothing is as it should be. It makes thinking difficult too, the deep wash of the bar, it dissolves her mind. Her brain feels water-damaged, saturated, full of bilge. If she could wring it out perhaps she could comprehend this place, these things she does, her situation. She has to concentrate hard on any task, sweeping up broken crockery, taking an order from a customer, putting money into the register. She has to try hard not to float away completely. When she looks down from the dark end of the bar the light in front of the windows is abundant and always shifting. It glimmers and bounces and flickers delicately, fooling the eyes and distorting depth perception, as if it has arrived through a layer of something in perpetual motion, something refractive and untrustworthy, something massive and unending.

The bar room itself it tidal. It ebbs and flows, morning and night, is busy and then quiet again. When the crowds recede the place is littered full of jetsam and flotsam, crumpled packets and wrappers, cigarette stubs left in ashtrays like crustacean segments, plates of food pecked at by scavengers. The tables are sticky and grainy as if salt deposits have been left along their rims, and the smooth glasses held against tap nozzles in the girl's hand feel as if they have been polished for a long time by the drag of water over shingle, buffed and un-roughened at their stems. There are dribbles and puddles everywhere, damp patches on the floor, and the cleaning solution used for every surface has a strong green marine smell.

She has forgotten how long she has worked here exactly, in the hotel with its briny seascape rooms – the last building in its row on the street, where life swells up in waves against the border of settlement, passing fishmongers and alleyways and schools as it crests, then breaks, collecting in this strange end chamber of the old town. How long has she lived in this small place by the North Sea? A year? Ten years? Twenty? It seems like forever. She doesn't remember coming here, or the indefinite cause of it. Was it as a student? For a job? Was it love? Was it loss? Why did she stay? She wonders if she will ever leave, and how she could leave. The thought is exhausting, the solution elusive. All she can remember is this life, this existence. The work, the headaches, the apnea, the man at the corner table and her feelings of having to watch him down at the bottom of the ocean. And always the smell of sea. Life erases itself in this place as soon as it is lived, and she lets it go without fighting, knowing it will come back just the same. She is eroded, and redistributed, her whole being is tectonic. But for one clear memory she has at her centre, which has not worn away, and which she holds onto like a precious possession, even though it has become redundant, even though it is her last.

* * *

She remembers visiting this place when she was a small child. Her parents brought her to the town on holiday. Usually every summer they would go to one of the western isles, with beautiful sounding names, and beautiful red sunsets that her father said tugged the heart out to sea after them. But this year was different, her parents wanted a change, so they took an alternate turn and came to the east coast instead where the sea was much colder and darker and it had the desolate spirit of the north in it, the sands were very fine, almost white, and the sun set at her back. It felt inside out. It felt a little like being on the wrong side. The sea was the sea was the sea, her parents said, it made no difference where you were, but she wasn't so sure. The town was heavy, pretty, with ancient walls and a quiet, reserved nature. It had an atmosphere of containment, sacrament, like a stone bowl, a chalice. They checked into a small hotel at the edge of one of the main streets and were shown to their rooms. Hers was small, with pictures of shells and boats on the walls, and from the window she could make out a blue head of water, between shoulders of brick. Then they had a meal in the bar downstairs.

The hotel was the last building in its row before the sturdy citadel wall with its thick arched doorways. It was not far from the shore, and the caw of gulls could be heard in the distance. She asked her parents if she could collect shells on the beach the next day and they said it would be fine. But for four days there was a haar so thick along the coast nothing could be seen, fog rolled up into the town like the grey, pneumonic breath of the sea, so they looked in souvenir shops and museums, and climbed the cathedral tower which gave a view of nothing but cloud and mist. When the weather was poor, her mother said it made her bones feel as if they had been set badly, as if they weren't joined up properly, so they didn't walk too far. After they had explored the visible town they strolled up and down the hotel's street, aimlessly, and it began to seem claustrophobic and smaller each time. They bought white bony fish from the blue tiled fish shop half way down the road, which was brought down from the smoke huts further up the coast each day. The smokies came wrapped in white paper with their price pencilled on the package, and their flavour was rich, delicately rancid. They took it back to the hotel and ate it with brown bread and butter, without being hungry. Her parents let her pull up the tanned skin and remove plump flakes of it from the spine with her fingers. When they had done everything they felt they could in the town they stayed in the hotel and played cards in the bar room. The place seemed murky and dull, it had a strange sense of loneliness and isolation. Even when it rained on the west coast it was not so sombre or so desolate as this, she thought. She watched the bar staff conveying wares to customers and wiping counters. Each seemed busy and not really willing to speak to her, and when they stopped work they stared off into space. She felt stuck inside and bored, sitting at the corner table with her cheek on her fist while her parents read the paper. Each day her mother would say the weather forecast looked better for tomorrow and they would surely be able to go out to the shore. And each day the haar remained. It was like the holiday would never begin and never end.

Then on the fifth day the fog was gone. When she woke up the sun was shining in through a gap in the curtains, and as she looked out she could see the last trails of it being sucked out to sea, into the open mouth of the horizon, like smoke inhaled by a great lung. Everything seemed light and shiny and full of possibility. After breakfast her mother and father equipped her with a plastic bucket and a bamboo fishing rod with a net on the end and walked with her down to the castle. The smaller of the town's two beaches lay just beyond it. They told her she could go down and explore, they were going to look at the castle and would not be gone too long. They told her to be careful and she promised she would. They would come and find her soon, they said, and then they would all go to the bigger sands together afterwards, where they might see some seals. In an emergency she should go back to the hotel and wait for them. They repeated this final instruction and she nodded and said she understood.

The steps down to the beach were steep and tilted and sprinkled with sand, hard to manage in her plastic beach shoes, so she held on to the wall for balance. At the bottom she turned and waved to her parents, and they made their way into the castle grounds. Down below, the tide was out, and the sand was rippled and ridged, swept into patterns. Everything had a pungent seaweed smell. She moved along the lip of the water checking for shells and found several broken pink pieces which she put in her pocket. To the left, a broad shoulder of rock was exposed, with rungs of fissures like a ladder to climb up. She threw her net and bucket up onto the boulder and dug her toes into the brackets of rock, lifting herself up. Beyond was a large stony outcrop that ran round underneath the castle ruins, made up of little ridges and summits, pools and rivulets, and half in shadow from the angle of the late morning sun.

It was strewn with the residue of the tide, things ground down, rent and uprooted, and moved from where they originally belonged. The scent of kelp and the reek of the ocean were stronger here, like an uncleared table with the sea's offerings left out to ripen and decay. There was a messy feel to this part of the beach, as if it required tidying. She picked up the fishing net and bucket and made her way carefully across the slippery, uneven ground towards the first of the pools, careful not to trap her foot in any of the crevices, the seaweed taut and glossy like wet cartilage under her heels. The pool was an unfriendly gully with some crabs' legs broken and scattered untidily around its edges. She knelt down on a ribbon of bubbled fabric covering the ground and put her hand into the water. It was chilled, dark, lifeless. The sunlight had not yet warmed it. She stood and moved further out on the apron of rock, her feet sliding over sleek pods and small red jellyfish. She looked back. The soft ruffled sands could no longer be seen, she was now at the hard jawbone of the North Sea. In front of her was a larger pool, shallower than the last but much broader, with ripples on its surface from a channel that let seawater come sliding gently in and out, the tide at its lowest hinging point. It was at the exact point where the cusp of shadow lay across the beach. The sun was sparkling in one corner of pool. And at the other, darker end, resting across the rock like another piece of organic debris, was a man.

She thought then about calling out, her parents might be able to hear her from the castle if she shouted loudly enough and they would rush to find her, turn her away, comfort her and tell her to forget what she had seen. But she was not scared. There was no panic in her. This was a rare find, special, and it was not frightening. She looked at the corpse; it was a man that was no longer just a man, he had been changed by the hold of the sea, by travelling with its motion for some time. He had been bleached and blanched by the water and his clothing was almost as colourless as his swollen flesh. His back and legs must have been broken because he was lying in a sharp but loose position that almost folded him in two, half in and half out of the pool, bent closely across a large stone, like the compliant, pulpy marine vegetation all around him. One boot was gone and the other was gaping at the laces. His face was bloated white and splitting dark brown at the edges, like a swollen mushroom cap. It was completely underwater. The skin looked old and withered but also freer, translucent, emulsified, as if it was now the hide of a sea animal, an anatomy used to the lilt and drift of its environment.

The girl paused for a moment and then made her way cautiously along the edge of the pool towards the body. She sat down and put her feet in the water next to it, leaned over and looked carefully. The face was fascinating. The eye sockets had expanded and looked puffy but the lids were still open. They were still open as if in greeting. Hello, hello, little girl. It seemed to her that the man's eyes had somehow become joined with the water. They were now made of the sea. They escaped his face, folding backwards and forwards into the surrounding liquid, which moved with the tide slightly as if the man's breath was blowing it. Their damp shine was the glint of the brine in which they were kept. She met their gaze. He did not seem dead.

This pool itself was full of life. Pale, almost invisible shrimp pedalled about just under the surface, spinning around and crawling over the man's cheeks. There were orange antennae protruding from hidden shelves, fragile and alert, ready to retreat at the smallest of movements, a slight change in the atmospheric pressure. A school of tiny silvery fish hung in the water next to the man's earlobe. His hair curled with the sea anemones as the residue and return of the current agitated between the rock walls. A few barnacles had attached themselves to his belt, his shirt had come untucked from his trousers, it was twisted up against his chest, and his belly was exposed. Only two of its buttons remained fastened, two more were open and one was lost. Underneath, his torso had ballooned with liquid, saturating itself in the terrain, adjusting to its new home out at sea. She felt sure if she were to run her hands along the man's ribcage or spine she would find scales growing between the valleys of bone. He was almost not human now. He was a halfling. When she went back, she thought, she would tell her parents that she had found a merman. She should probably find them now, but she couldn't take her eyes off him.

After a little while she became aware that the odour of marine leftovers and waste was at its strongest here. If only the body had stayed in the water instead of arriving up on the shoreline it might have been changed completely into something else and not begun to decompose. He might have been adopted and given another life. But the man had been tossed up on land like he was unwanted, he had been forgotten about and was spoiling, he was like an old rotting fish that should be wrapped in newspaper and thrown away. She watched his rocking, floating face. He was so curious amid the ordinary leavings of the ocean, so different, familiar but alien. Something between worlds. Vulnerable. She felt he must be seen to, cared for. She knew she couldn't do this alone, she couldn't pull him out of the pool or push him into the waves to be taken back out to sea, he looked too heavy and was fastened too tightly to the rocks. She wasn't sure what she could do.

The tide was coming back in, she could feel it flooding slowly and insistently against her ankles. The sea might want him back after all, easing him out of the grip of the beach and gently into its belly where all taken things were suspended, and remade. He would become finished. But before it took him away again perhaps she could help him a little. She would undo his buttons that were closed, the ones that were still attached to the colourless shirt, so that he could slip out of the clothing easier and continue to grow scales, or become encrusted with salt creatures. She squatted down over the body and put her hands on his chest and the little school of fish by his head flickered away to the other end of the pool. The man was the exact temperature of the water, no warmer. The wool of the shirt was sodden and would not cooperate. The material was too stiff to manipulate, too steeped by salty liquid, and the buttons were fraught and feeble, anxious about leaving their holes. Her fingers felt too weak and numb. She kept fumbling, and looking away from the drowned cloth that she was working on and at the man's sea-eyes, waving hello to her, and it seemed a long time since she had seen another face but his. The sun was moving across the pool, its rays reflecting with blinding brilliance.

Her parents had not yet come to find her, but she knew she was far round on the outcrop, beyond the beach, and they might have missed her. Perhaps they had gone back to the hotel to wait for her after all. Perhaps this place, this dead man, counted as an emergency like they had said. Small waves began to break inside the chamber, disturbing the calm of the water and obscuring the body underneath. After a few moments she could not make out the form anymore, its image came apart and dissolved under the gathering churn of the bore. She could feel the buttons between her fingers, stubborn, and impossible to release. She did not want to leave him this way. It seemed important not to. Then she heard somebody call her name, a voice that seemed both close by and distant at once. She straightened up and looked around the apron of rock but she could see no-one who might have spoken to her. A wave broke against her legs, washing up her back to her neck. For the first time she felt the absolute coldness of the North Sea, the icy surge of it. The level of the water in the pool had risen quickly since she first found it, reaching further over the man than before, drenching his legs again, and sweeping under his broken shape. The body was beginning to dislodge in the current, peeling up off the ground. She felt a hand suddenly come alive in the tide and brush past her ankle. It was time to go. She turned to put her foot on the side of the rock pool to pull herself out, and it skidded off and splashed back down. The spray of the sea had turned the walls of the enclosure into slick shining surfaces. She tried again, stepping higher and using her cold hands to haul herself upwards. But again her shoe slipped from the ledge as she began to climb. She felt herself falling backwards and her head hit a piece of rock behind her with the dull sound of something snapping underwater. Then she heard her name called again, fainter this time.

ANDREW LANG

Almae Matres

(St Andrews, 1862. Oxford, 1865)

St Andrews by the Northern Sea,
A haunted town it is to me!
A little city, worn and grey,
The grey North Ocean girds it round,
And o'er the rocks, and up the bay,
The long sea-rollers surge and sound.
And still the thin and biting spray
Drives down the melancholy street,
And still endure, and still decay,
Towers that the salt winds vainly beat.
Ghost-like and shadowy they stand
Dim mirrored in the wet sea-sand.

St Leonard's chapel, long ago
We loitered idly where the tall
Fresh-budded mountain ashes blow
Within thy desecrated wall:
The tough roots rent the tomb below,
The April birds sang clamorous,
We did not dream, we could not know
How hardly Fate would deal with us!

O, broken minster, looking forth
Beyond the bay, above the town,
O, winter of the kindly North,
O, college of the scarlet gown,
And shining sands beside the sea,
And stretch of links beyond the sand,
Once more I watch you, and to me
It is as if I touched his hand!

And therefore art thou yet more dear,
O, little city, grey and sere,
Though shrunken from thine ancient pride
And lonely by thy lonely sea,
Than these fair halls on Isis' side,
Where Youth and hour came back to me!
A land of waters green and clear,
Of willow and of poplars tall,
And, in the spring-time of the year,
The white may breaking over all,
And Pleasure quick to come at call.
And summer rides by marsh and wold,
And Autumn with her crimson pall
About the towers of Magdalen rolled;
And strange enchantments from the past,
And memories of the friends of old,
And strong Tradition, binding fast
The 'flying terms' with bands of gold, –
All these hath Oxford: all are dear,
But dearer far the little town,
The drifting surge, the wintry year,
The college of the scarlet gown.
St Andrews by the Northern Sea,
That is a haunted town to me!

ROBERT LOUIS STEVENSON

The Gem of the Province

And but a little way round the corner of the land, imminent itself above the sea, stands the gem of the province and the light of mediaeval Scotland, St Andrews, where the great Cardinal Beaton held garrison against the world, and the second of the name and title perished (as you may read in Knox's jeering narrative) under the knives of true-blue Protestants, and to this day (after so many centuries) the current voice of the professor is not hushed.

DOUGLAS YOUNG

Haybox, Hoopoe, Gold

In 1882 W. C. McIntosh, Professor of Natural History (1882–1916), started work in an improvised laboratory consisting of a timber fever-hospital by the East Sands. In 1896 he was provided with the Gatty Marine Laboratory, through the generosity of an Englishman, Dr C. H. Gatty, and much valuable work was done for fisheries. St Andrews still had about a hundred fishermen with fourteen boats in mid-Victorian times. McIntosh was born in 1838, the year when the small medieval red gown was lengthened and sleeved to make a student's cloak. He died in 1931. Even in his nineties he was to be seen working at the Gatty, wearing his old red gown, and sometimes with his feet in a hay-box to keep them warm. His successor, Sir D'Arcy Wentworth Thompson, went to Dundee as professor in 1884, aged twenty-four, and held the Chair of Natural History at St Andrews from 1917 to 1948, when he died, having been sixty-four years a professor. Best known for his epoch-making book *Growth and Form*, D'Arcy had the widest-ranging of interests, and wrote, *inter alia*, glossaries of ancient Greek birds and fishes. When a hoopoe was shot on the golf-course in autumn 1930, D'Arcy took it about, wrapped in a silk handkerchief, and discoursed to his classes on Aristophanes' *Birds*. At graduations, when Principal Irvine made false quantities in his Latin, D'Arcy could be heard making strange whoops and whistles from behind his majestic beard, a beard the prickliness of which was attested by pretty bejantines with whom he danced in the 1930s, when he was in his seventies.

* * *

In one of their agitations, in 1912, the West Fife miners sent a squad of muscular colliers, equipped with stout sticks, to go round the mansions of the St Andrews *rentiers* and ask for contributions to the strike fund. The comfortable denizens of Hepburn Gardens and elsewhere mostly handed over some golden sovereigns, rather than risk having their lawns dug up at night or their conservatories bombarded with stones. Andrew Lang had been living largely in St Andrews since 1891, and was growing old. The advent of the miners terrified him. He buried all his coined gold in the garden, and fled to Banchory on Deeside, where he succumbed to a heart-attack. His wife testified, 'It was really the strikes that killed him.' It is said that nobody ever found his hidden cash.

ROBERT CRAWFORD

D'Arcy

He wore an old jacket because his passenger
Liked to claw and bill into the tweed.

As he passed along South Street towards the Owl House
Children brought dead birds, shocking him

By not knowing their names – chaffinch, *fringilla coelebs;*
Cinclus cinclus, dipper or water ousel. Once a storm

Blew the pinioned lime-green wings across three gardens.
'Professor Thompson wants his parrot back.'

He wore it home. It spoke. It sang his name,
'D'Arcy, D'Arcy,' as he wrote his thesis

On form in evolution, cackling and sipping
Sometimes a dram, or a glass of Hirondelle.

TOM SCOTT

from *Brand the Builder*

The Toun Hall carved abuin its porch
Is hard bye, fit for dances, boxin,
Concerts, plays and the darg o cooncillors
Efter the day's caain in o siller
In their bits o shops and ither businesses,
And no faur hyne the Secondary Schuil
Madras College, set in its ain park
Ahent the ruins o a bleck friars' chapel.
East again, St Mary's, throu its pend
The Charles's oak wi its twa-three fantail doos
Forenenst the Bute wi D'Arcy's braw museum
Rowth o birds, beasts and fish, and ither
Zoological treisures, in drawers, and cases,
And its paintit porch wi the awesome bible quote
'They that go down to the sea in ships and do
Business in the great waters, thcsc men
See the works of the Lord and His wonders in
The mighty deep' sounds an organ chord.

* * *

The herbour crooks its lang and stany airms
Aboot a hantle o cobles, hauds the sea
At bay, pushes it back at Norroway,
Nae langer a bield of herrin fleets and sic,
Its fisher fowk, crusty's their ain crustacea,
Cleared langsyne inti cooncil hooses
Whaur they cannae even hear the seuch o the swaw,
Like partans, labsteers, strandit by the tide.
And at nicht the Plew, Pleiades and Orion
Keep the coorse they keepit in Bruce's time

Ay, and a million years afore Sant Aundrae
Follaed a chiel in white roond Galilee ...

* * *

      For the young fowk o the toun there's little choice
When they leave the schuil, but to leave the toun as weill
And seek a livin in the faaen world
Furth o Sant Aundraes, for there's little here
That can employ aucht but the simplest talents
In a wee toun o tradesmen and their ilk,
Shopkeepers, hoteliers and little else.
The ablest o the young maun seek professions
In the big cities – Dundee for some,
But maist land up in Glesca, Edinburgh,
Manchester, London, Canada, Australia
And siclike airts. I mysel hae met
A schuildays' freend doctorin on the Niger.
Whit fowk are left are aa ye need to hae
To service St Leonards and the 'Varsity
And the aged Aberglaube o retired colonels
Commanders, Indian (or ither) Civil Servants,
A few o them hame to dee whaur they were born
In the toun they were forced to leave when they were young.
Nae wonder it's a toun hauntit by
Nostalgie for a lost and loved Eden
(Even gin the 'Eden' is nocht but a gowf-coorse!)
A toun for bairns and the auld, and gey few atween.

EDWIN MORGAN

Thomas Young, M.A. (St Andrews)

For J.C.B.

'Yes, I taught Milton. He was a sharp boy.
He never understood predestination,
but then who does, within the English nation?
I did my best to let him see what joy
there must be in observing the damnation
of those whom God makes truly reprobate:
the fair percentage does not decreate
heaven, but gives all angels the elation
they are justly decreed to have deserved.
We took a short tour up to Auchterarder,
where there are strong sound sergeants of the creed,
but John could only ask how God was served
by those who neither stand nor wait, their ardour
rabid (he said) to expunge virtue's seed?'

Industry and the Slothful Herd

... Dr. Baird (whom you and I saw many years after at his native place, St Andrew's in Scotland) gave a contrary opinion: 'For the industry of that Franklin,' says he, 'is superior to any thing I ever saw of the kind; I see him still at work when I go home from club, and he is at work again before his neighbours are out of bed.' (*Autobiography*)

NOS UNIVERSITATIS ST. ANDREAE apud SCOTOS Rector Promotor, Collegiorum Praefecti, Facultatis Artium Decanus, caeterique Professorum Ordines, Lectoribus Salutem QUANDOQUIDEM aequum est et Rationi congruens, ut qui magno Studio bonas didicerunt Artes, iidem referant Praemium Studiis suis dignum, ac prae inerti Hominum vulgo propriis quibusdam fulgeant Honoribus et Privilegiis, unde et ipsis bene sit, atque aliorum provocetur Industria; QUANDO etiam eo praesertim spectant amplissima illa Jura Universitati Andreanae antiquibus concessa, ut, quoties respostulat, idoneos quosque in quavis facultate viros, vel Summis qui ad eam Facultatem pertinent, Honoribus amplificare queat;

We the Rector, Provost, Presidents of the Colleges, Dean of the Faculty of Arts, and other Orders of Professors in the University of St Andrews in Scotland, to our Readers Greeting. Whereas it is just and reasonable, that they who by great Study have learned the Arts, should also receive a Reward worthy of their Studies, and outshine the slothful Herd of Mankind by some peculiar Honours and Privileges, both to reward them and excite the Industry of others; And whereas the Design of those very extensive Privileges granted in ancient times to the University of St. Andrews is, that as oft as Occasion requires they have it in their Power to dignify Men excelling in any Faculty with the highest Honours appertaining to

QUUMQUE ingenuus et honestus Vir BENJAMINUS FRANKLIN, Artium Magister, non solum Jurisprudentiae Cognitione, Morum Integritate, Suavique Vitae Consuetudine, Nobis sit commendatus, Verum etiam, acute inventus, et exitu felici factis Experimentis, quibus Rerum Naturalium, et imprimis Rei Electricae parum hactenus exploratae, Scientiam locupletavit, tantum sibi conciliaverit per Orbem Terrarum Laudem, ut summus in Republica Literaria mereatur Honores: Hisce nos adducti, et praemia Virtuti debita, quantum in nobis est, tribuere volentes, Magistrum BEN-JAMINUM FRANKLIN supra nominatum, UTRIUSQUE JURIS DOCTOREM Creamus, Constituimus et Renunciamus Eumque deinceps ab universis pro Doctore dignissimo haberi volumus; adjicimusque Ei, plena manu, quaecunque uspiam gentium. Juris utriusque Doctoribus competunt Privilegia et Ornamenta. In cuius Rei testimonium hasce nostras Privilegii, Literas,

that Faculty; and whereas the ingenuous and worthy Benj: Franklin has not only been recommended to us for his Knowledge of the Law, the Rectitude of his Morals and Sweetness of his Life and Conversation, but hath also by his ingenious Inventions and successful Experiments with which he hath enriched the Science of natural Philosophy and more especially of Electricity which heretofore was little known, acquired so much Praise throughout the World as to deserve the greatest Honours in the Republic of Letters; For these Reasons and from a willingness as far as in us lies to bestow the Rewards due to Virtue we create constitute and declare the above named Mr. Benjamin Franklin Doctor of Laws and will that for the future he be treated by all as the most Worthy Doctor, and we grant to him with a liberal Hand all the Privileges and Honours, which are any where granted to Doctors of Laws. In Testimony of which we have given these our

Chirographis singulorum confirmatas, et communi Almae Universitatis Sigillo munitas DEDIMUS ANDREAPOLI duodecimo Die Mensis Februarii Anno Domini millesimo Septingentesimo quinquagesimo nono.

Letters signed with our Hands and sealed with the common Seal of the University at St Andrews the 12th of February 1759.

AND. SHAW S.T.P. Univers. Rector et Promotor

THOS. TULLIDEPH Coll: St. Salvat: et St. Leonar: Praefectus

JA. MURISON Coll. Mar: Praefectus

ROBTUS WATSON P.P. Fac. Art. Doc.

THOMAS SIMSON Med. et Anat. p. candosensis

DAVID YOUNG P.P.

JOANNES YOUNG P.P.

DAVID GREGORIE Math: P.

GUIEL: BROWN S.T. et H.E.P.

ALEXR. MORTON H.L.P.

GUAL. WILSON G.L.P.

GEOR: HADOW M.D. Ling. Heb. P.

The March Stone

The march between the Shanwell and Old Muirs salmon fishing is in a straight line from the top of Norman's Law to the low water. This march stone stands in said straight line. 1794

Fishing Marker, Tentsmuir Forest, Eden & Tay Estuaries, Fife

Take time to stand here by the stone, feel
the sandy loam go down for yards beneath
your boots, and listen to the silence,
to the susurrus of sea somewhere away

to east, where this line threads its route
through pines, through marram grass,
across the dune slack, all the shrugged up
sandhills of the coast to zero ground,

sea level, where it makes its mark, imagined
on the wet sand of the beach: a terminus
determined by the law. And this time turn
to west, search keenly through the trunks,

the tangle of the forest, for that hill
whose shape you think you know but
cannot recognise, the one these picked out
words say marks the farther end of this,

the dimly minded boundary one stone
has been erected to maintain. Imagine it,
invisible but paid out in the thought
of netsmen, pilots, players of the line

they wound from pole to pole, just as
this border knots each bield and brae face
straight – the way a gull flies inland –
heading for the summit of the Law

these trees grew up to hide. One stone,
its legend carved for anyone to read,
that must have stood close to the shore
two centuries ago, before the sands moved,

changed the angle of the coast, took fish
and men away, to argue other boundaries,
seek a different Eden, out beyond the Tay,
beyond the lines of memory, underway.

JOHN BURNSIDE

History

St Andrews: West Sands; September 2001

Today
     as we flew the kites
– the sand spinning off in ribbons along the beach
and that gasoline smell from Leuchars gusting across
the golf links;
           the tide far out
and quail-grey in the distance;
                   people
jogging, or stopping to watch
as the war planes cambered and turned
in the morning light –

today
     – with the news in my mind, and the muffled dread
of what may come –

              I knelt down in the sand
with Lucas
     gathering shells
and pebbles
        finding evidence of life in all this
driftwork:
        snail shells; shreds of razorfish;
smudges of weed and flesh on tideworn stone.

At times I think what makes us who we are
is neither kinship nor our given states
but something lost between the world we own
and what we dream about behind the names
on days like this

                    our lines raised in the wind
our bodies fixed and anchored to the shore

and though we are confined by property
what tethers us to gravity and light
has most to do with distance and the shapes
we find in water
                        reading from the book
of silt and tides
                        the rose or petrol blue
of jellyfish and sea anemone
combining with a child's
first nakedness.

Sometimes I am dizzy with the fear
of losing everything – the sea, the sky,
all living creatures, forests, estuaries:
we trade so much to know the virtual
we scarcely register the drift and tug
of other bodies
                        scarcely apprehend
the moment as it happens: shifts of light
and weather
                        and the quiet, local forms
of history: the fish lodged in the tide
beyond the sands;
                        the long insomnia
of ornamental carp in public parks

captive and bright
                      and hung in their own
slow-burning
           transitive gold;
                           jamjars of spawn
and sticklebacks
               or goldfish carried home
from fairgrounds
               to the hum of radio

but this is the problem: how to be alive
in all this gazed-upon and cherished world
and do no harm

                 a toddler on a beach
sifting wood and dried weed from the sand
and puzzled by the pattern on a shell

his parents on the dune slacks with a kite
plugged into the sky
                  all nerve and line

patient; afraid; but still, through everything
attentive to the irredeemable.

DON PATERSON

Old Man Under an Apple Tree, East Scores

after Quasimodo

I will know nothing of my life but its mysteries,
the dead cycles of the breath and sap.
I shall not know whom I loved, or love,
now that in the random winds of March
with nothing but my limbs, I draw into myself
and the years counted deep in me.
The thin blossom is already streaming from the boughs.
I watch the pure calm of its only flight.

HUGH MacDIARMID

An Ideal Forum

Mention should ... be made here of Mr J. H. Whyte's 'Abbey Bookshop'
in St Andrews – the only really European bookshop in Great Britain
with the exception of Bumpus's in Oxford Street, London (which, *nota
bene*, is also run by a Scotsman, Mr J. G. Wilson). Mr Whyte has
admirably reconstructed the interior of this fine sixteenth-century
house, and here all the important books and periodicals of Europe can
be seen as they appear. It is already becoming a focus for all the active
intellectual interest in Scotland – an ideal forum of all the vital tenden-
cies in Internationalism and Scottish Nationalism alike.

The Home of "The Modern Scot"

Today, on this blustery, autumn-tinted afternoon in 2004, I stand once more before the entrance to No 3, South Street, St Andrews, well-nigh seventy years since I first came to know the place, though the massive doorway with its impregnable iron strappings still appears unchanged, frowning upon the stranger with a decided air of ownership.

In 1935, however, my sister, Francise and I had no misgivings as to what lay behind this bulwark of antiquity as we strolled by way of the Roundel and into South Street on our way to window-shopping or other innocent teenage diversions. Across the entire edifice, its façade a mighty jumble of heaved-up stones weathered to alternating greys and blacks held together by bleached dabs of mortar, one could trace the erosive hand of centuries unloading searing East Coast storms, catastrophes of plagues and burnings amid the suggestive whiff of incense and inquisition lingering by the abbey wall. My mother and father had brought us to this place. My mother was Burges Gray, from Aberdeenshire, and my father the composer, Francis George Scott.

In 1926 the Scott family (exiled to Glasgow from my parents' native Hawick and Fraserburgh by reason of my father's lectureship at Jordanhill Teachers' Training College) went on holiday to St Cyrus on the Kincardineshire coast. At St Cyrus the Scotts met my father's former pupil and now adult friend Christopher Murray Grieve, best remembered as the poet Hugh MacDiarmid. Grieve and his family were enjoying a two-month respite from his journalist's duties in nearby Montrose. By 1928 the Scott family decided on Montrose as their next holiday destination, a plan which led to meetings with Edwin and Willa Muir (Willa's parents were owners of a draper's shop on the High Street), and the family of Christopher Grieve, Peggy his wife, and the first of his children, Christine. The end of the twenties saw the Scott family at Kilcreggan, but my father, disheartened by the steady Clydeside downpour, decreed that we go off to St Andrews – this in 1931 – where we obtained lodging with a Mrs Robertson on South Street. By 1932 we were staying at Beethoven Lodge, North Street, then the property of three Henderson sisters, later converted to house the University Printing Department. By now James H. Whyte (to whom MacDiarmid would later dedicate his poem 'On a Raised Beach') was publishing some of my father's songs in his 'Modern Scot', a literary journal first published in 1930, and remarkable as much for its presentation as for its literary content. In his book *The Modern Scot* (2000) Dr Tom Normand has written in detail about Whyte and his work. By the time I knew him Whyte was already publishing in *The Modern Scot* work by W. H. Auden, Paul Eluard, Neil Gunn, Herman Hesse, Franz Kafka, Eric Linklater, Hugh MacDiarmid, Compton Mackenzie, Naomi Mitchison, Edwin Muir, and many other writers, artists, composers, and intellectuals. At this time St Andrews was fast becoming a centre for the so-called 'Scottish Renaissance', a term first used by one of its strongest adherents, Denis Saurat (a close friend of my father), in the article 'Le Groupe de la "Renaissance Ecossaise", 1924'.

The year 1935 and succeeding years saw us spending school and college holidays at No 5 North Street, the former coastguard building converted by Whyte into an art gallery on the top floor at that point adjoining the adjacent flat at No 11, the address of Whyte's friend, colleague and partner John Tonge who used the pseudonym 'A. T. Cunningham' for his aesthetic writings. On the Scores, just a stone's throw from the North Street house and facing the sea and castle, stood the villa of 'Castlelea', at that period the home of Edwin and Willa Muir and their young son, Gavin. The house still looks out on the medieval ruins which were to become the subject of Edwin's poem 'The Castle'.

As a very young teenager, I found my first job, unpaid, of course, in Whyte's art gallery. I remember looking round the gallery and being offered the job as receptionist, the kind of work I enjoyed. Down in the entrance hall stood a very interesting sculpture by Loris Ray. It had the rounded, smooth planes characteristic of Ray's work. The public used to come nosing through the front arched doorway of the entrance just to look at this and then sneak out again. Everybody wondered what was behind these doors. There was a great air of mystery about the whole place. James, who occasionally collided with inquirers who would ask him to explain the statue, said, 'I do believe it might be "Mother and Child"'.

Being part of this St Andrews artistic community was a totally exhilarating experience for my sister and me (Francise was four years older than me and much at home on the social scene). And at seventeen the whole exciting world lay open before me – with an intangible air of mystery about the place (whether more noticeable in St Andrews than elsewhere or a mirage of youthful imaginings). But already rumours of war wafted around the hallowed steeples of the old Grey City, leaving a faint impression that they were in some way connected with the tenant of No 3 South Street. An overloaded Mercedes Benz had been spotted arriving in the vicinity of Nos 5 and 11 North Street and of course the whole populace were quick to associate this happening with the presence of certain 'mystery' characters, 'connected no doubt with the University' and occasionally glimpsed in the darker byways of the town. But the main focus of the investigations of these good St Andreans fell on the tenant of No 3, the owner of the Abbey Book Shop – 'there were some queer ongoings in there, right enough'. Who would have imagined such cantraips in these surroundings, today doucely converted to a students' residence and study centre?

Of course Francise and I were delighted to find ourselves at no loss for entertaining company: to single out J. H. Whyte, he was not only owner/editor/proprietor of the Abbey Book Shop but together with abounding business acumen he had an attractive manner in his approach to people, being thoroughly at ease in society. He was from time to time the generous host at evenings which were literary or musical, or more often a mix of both, entertaining fresh arrivals of what appeared to be total strangers from all points of the compass. Our own holiday house on North Street was already a delightful haven for our friends to whom we offered hospitality for a short stay. So this highly social lifestyle continued between three houses: 'Castlelea' on the Scores, our house on North Street, and the Whyte residence on South Street.

A closer view of these houses and their tenants reveals something of their character. The North Street house had been referred to in the 1930s by local people as 'a Moorish Monstrosity'. It was modelled on the Bauhaus avant-garde school of architecture, its interior furnishings of the most outré design, having much closer affinity to the then developing European styles than anything yet offered in these Northern parts. The number 5 which we occupied had more than a trace of Germanic influence in its décor and wall hangings and the canvases adorning its walls. It was here that I first saw examples of the work of Paul Klee, lining the staircase walls – there were numerous examples of his prints and I believe some original items. The house was occupied by and rented out to William Stewart of the French Department, whose wife was German.

Among the visitors whom we met at this time might be mentioned Dr Oscar Oeser, then, in the period from 1935–40 lecturer in Experimental Psychology at the university. He was in the course of expounding the latest in up-to-date theories in the realm of psychology; obviously the ideas of Nietzsche, Hegel, Freud and Jung held great appeal for the younger generation of the time and lofty discussions abounded in this new field of research at the parties hosted by J. H. Whyte in his South Street house. 'Mind Games' were all the rage and appeared as a highly developed form of mind-reading – a pastime for which Willa Muir had a particular penchant, having a special interest in the workings of the human mind. Her conclusions were often reached as the result of her studying the latest theories on, for example, bringing up children, and so convinced was she that her psychology manuals held the answer to almost any problem, she was often disillusioned when her conclusions turned out to be unreliable. Of course her husband, Edwin, had a similar, near-obsessive interest in these contemporary concepts in psychology evidenced in much of his prose and poetry. This social scene included a St Andrews artist, S. D. Horne Shepherd who with his young wife, Flossie, adorned the parties for a while – but perhaps they were only passing through the town. William Jeffrey, the poet, I also recall. He was considered a good poet, a view I still hold, though he was badly incapacitated by a severe stammer. My father set some of his early lyrics to music. My father's cousin William Johnstone also graced the South Street parties with his wife, the American artist, Flora. He was later to become Head of London Central School of Art, and produced some outstanding books on art in education. Most importantly, he produced canvases of remarkable interest, such as *A Point in Time* (1929–38), which earned for him a place of distinction in modern painting.

Among aspiring writers of this period should be mentioned George Bruce, nephew of my mother, and, like his aunt, hailing from Fraserburgh. He was soon to blaze a trail in the élite world of literary achievement, especially in his poetry. His work as a poet flourished alongside a successful broadcasting career. I remember too the presence of a Mr Mathers who assisted in the Abbey Book Shop: he had some connection with the earliest version of the Byre Theatre, if I am not mistaken.

The Abbey Book Shop itself had a charming frontage on the ground floor at 3 South Street, with small bottle-glass windows flanking the massive, iron-studded door. Whyte, who might be called an American although he was the son of a Belgian Baroness, commenced the business selling not only secondhand books, but also first editions, and then original paintings. Many of these were brought in from Europe, appealing to an élite clientele. Writing in *The Scottish Educational Journal*, Hugh MacDiarmid sang the Abbey Book Shop's praises in 1931. Today, quiet reigns over the academic pavements outside and I suspect that drastic changes to the building have wreaked a profound transformation. But for me, long years ago, taking my infant steps all the way up to the Roundel, this was a secret pathway leading to a haven for writers, artists, musicians, a busy hive at the centre of the Scottish cultural scene – this, the home of 'The Modern Scot'.

EDWIN MUIR

The Castle

All through that summer at ease we lay,
And daily from the turret wall
We watched the mowers in the hay
And the enemy half a mile away.
They seemed no threat to us at all.

For what, we thought, had we to fear
With our arms and provender, load on load,
Our towering battlements, tier on tier,
And friendly allies drawing near
On every leafy summer road.

Our gates were strong, our walls were thick,
So smooth and high, no man could win
A foothold there, no clever trick
Could take us, have us dead or quick.
Only a bird could have got in.

What could they offer us for bait?
Our captain was brave and we were true ...
There was a little private gate,
A little wicked wicket gate.
The wizened warder let them through.

Oh then our maze of tunnelled stone
Grew thin and treacherous as air.
The cause was lost without a groan,
The famous citadel overthrown,
And all its secret galleries bare.

How can this shameful tale be told?
I will maintain until my death
We could do nothing, being sold;
Our only enemy was gold,
And we had no arms to fight it with.

Silvered with Stars

At first things looked as if they were going to turn out well for us at St Andrews. We liked the terrace house James Whyte had taken for us, on top of the cliffs beside the Castle, with the North Sea at our front door instead of a garden. Edwin wrote to the manager of our London bank asking for an overdraft and got it. An intelligent and sympathetic woman doctor, Dorothy Douglas, took me in hand and fixed me up so that I could at least carry on. Everything was within easy reach, a school for Gavin, shops, ancient ruins and pleasant walks by the sea. We had only to come to terms with it all, and first with James Whyte, his book-shop and his magazine, *The Modern Scot.*

We went to dine with James in his house, an old one in South Street thoroughly modernized inside. It was padded everywhere with cushions; the sitting-room ceiling had been painted blue to match them and silvered with stars. James was obviously a young man who liked to be in the fashion and could afford it; ceilings like his must have then been 'the fashion', and walls outfacing each other in contrasting colours. After dinner we heard a Sibelius symphony on his gramophone, for Sibelius was in the fashion too; we did not know the symphony and felt, as we told each other later, that we were being ushered into a whole new world, since in James's house the furniture, the pictures, the lighting, as well as the music, were all fashionably *avant-garde.*

James himself was self-conscious but kindly, and arranged for us to visit his shop and look at his two new houses. The shop had been ingen-iously constructed out of a barrel-vaulted room on the ground floor of another old building, a little farther along South Street. Both his house and the shop, seen from outside, were built in a traditional Scottish style with stones somewhat rough and full of character, carefully restored, a credit to their new owner. The barrel-vaulting inside the shop made an attractive setting for books, but its old-world atmosphere was startlingly contradicted by a fresco that faced one on entering; beside the end of the counter there was a large caricature of John Knox astride a beer-cask, raising high a reaming tankard, recognizably John Knox although he had a raddled nose and a wicked leer.

'We thought the young people would like it,' said James, a little peevishly, 'but the St Leonards girls have been forbidden to enter the shop.' The fresco had been suggested by his right-hand satellite, John, whom we had not yet met. So far, James complained, very few students had come in. Perhaps when term began again more of them would venture.

The shelves were impressively well stocked, and on the counter all the most modern magazines from France and the United States were laid out, together with a copy of nearly every book one had seen recently reviewed. Only customers were lacking ...

* * *

As a student I had not been aware of social stratification in the town, although the tendency may have existed, and there had been little of it in the University. Nowadays things were different. This I learned from Dr Drury Oeser, whose husband Oscar had just been made head of the new Psychology Department. Drury, herself a doctor of psychology and fresh from Cambridge, passed on to me her astonishment at the rigid protocol observed in the University. When she was out shopping on her bicycle, she said, and saw one of Oscar's research students, of course she waved to him in a friendly manner. But the students had privately begged her not to do so, pleading that they would get into trouble, since staff and students were not supposed to recognize each other in the street. She had also been told, by a professor's wife, that she should not have invited professors' wives and lecturers' wives to the same tea-party. Some of the Top Brass were simply awful, said Drury. One old professor had found a couple of Freud's books in the library, and swore they were covered with 'pornographic thumb-marks'.

* * *

The whole English Department, where we might have expected to meet some friendly interest, ignored us, taking its tone from the professor, who refused to admit that any contemporary work could be regarded as literature, or any contemporary writers as literary men. For Yeats he made an exception; he boasted that Yeats had once spent an afternoon on his sofa; but for an upstart like Edwin Muir, who was now labelled in the University as 'man who wrote for the papers' (so we were told), no exception could be made. Only the Oesers, the Greek Reader and one or two professors from the Divinity College of St Mary's were humanly friendly.

At first we were more amused than resentful. I remember a hilarious Sunday morning Edwin and I spent composing libellous clerihews about all the University high-hatters.

* * *

Our own new friends did not despise us for earning a living by writing, but they were interested in too many other things to have time left for modern literature. We found ourselves caught up in discussions on psychology, sociology, politics – most especially politics, the treachery of London politicians concerning the Spanish Civil War and Hitler's bullying demands in Europe … Many groups in St Andrews were at loggerheads. Between them, the University and St Leonards Girls' School were buying up or taking over more and more space for new buildings, acquiring more and more old buildings for reconstruction, and the townsfolk objected, complaining that they were being crowded out of their own town. In my time, the students living in town lodgings had formed a link between town and gown; the landladies took money from but also a possessive and maternal interest in their lodgers. Now that the students were confined to residential hostels the town made no direct profit out of them and there was huffy resentment among the townspeople. They were beginning also to dislike the Royal and Ancient Golf Club, since it was filling up with retired pro-consuls, mostly from India, who did their own shopping with large marketing bags and were heard in loud voices referring to the townsfolk as 'the natives'.

* * *

The War

The Professor of Greek, an elderly, thickset man, could be seen digging a trench on the hill above the pier, in shirt-sleeves and braces. More than anything else this brought home to one the change in St Andrews, where the menace of war had closed up the cracks in its social structure almost overnight. Edwin joined the Home Guard, one of a miscellaneous awkward squad including men of all classes, put through their drill by a tradesman who had been a sergeant-major in the first war. Shyly, almost furtively, in a corner of his study, using an old golf club instead of a rifle, Edwin practised the unfamiliar drill, and at night did sentry-go round the Telephone Exchange.

The fear of invasion by Germans, in the forefront of everyone's mind, made people consciously aware of the town they lived in, and because St Andrews was now important to their survival the townspeople were convinced that it was also important to Hitler and would be the first place he attacked. I should guess that in every town or village on the east coast of Britain people thought they would be Hitler's first target. What surprised me was that the intellectuals in the town were loudest in their prophecies of doom – even the Oesers. 'St Andrews will plastered,' they both said. 'It's only three miles from Leuchars aerodrome; of course it will be plastered with bombs. Simply plastered.'

* * *

Before we left for Edinburgh in 1942 St Andrews had its one and only bombing raid; a stick of four medium-sized bombs was dropped over some University buildings. The German plane flew very low with all lights on; we saw it not far above our roof, and the last bomb splintered our front door and its fanlight. No one was killed, by good chance, but various science buildings were much damaged. It looked as if some ex-student had indulged in a little private vengeance on the University.

WILLIAM DUNBAR

Sanct Salvatour!

from '*To the King*'

SANCT SALVATOUR! send silver sorrow;
It grevis me both evin and morrow,
Chasing fra me all cheritie;
It makis me all blythness to borrow;
My panefull purs so priclis me.

WALTER BOWER

The Founding of the University of St Andrews

translated by D. E. R. Watt from the Latin of the Scotichronicon

In the previous year (namely 1410) after Whitsunday an institution of higher learning of university standing made a start in the city of St Andrew of Kilrymont in Scotland when Henry de Wardlaw was the bishop of St Andrews and James Biset was the prior there. Master Laurence de Lindores (a great theologian and a man of respected life-style) was the first to begin lecturing there on the fourth book of the *Sentences*, Master Richard Cornell (a doctor of canon law and arch deacon of Lothian) on decrees, and sir John Litstar (a licentiate in decrees and canon of St Andrews) [a man of great knowledge of the religious life and of distinguished life-style] in the same faculty in the mornings. Subsequently Master John Scheves official of St Andrews and Master William Stephenson (who was later bishop of Dunblane) lectured in the same faculty, and Master John Gill, Master William Fowlis and Master William Croyser in philosophy and logic. They continued their lectures for two and a half years before the confirmation of the privileges [of the university]. At last in 1413 on 3 February (that is the morrow of the Purification of Our Lady, a Saturday, dominical letter F), the bearer of the privileges, Henry de Ogilvie M. A., arrived in the city of St Andrews. On his happy arrival a peal of all the [bells of the] city's churches was sounded. The next day, that is the following Sunday, at the ninth hour there was a formal meeting of all the clergy in the refectory (which had been specially fitted up for the occasion) when the bulls of privileges were presented to the lord bishop as chancellor of this gracious university. When the bulls had been read out before everybody, the clergy and convent processed to the high altar singing the *Te Deum laudamus* in harmonious voice. When this had been sung and everyone was on bended knee, the bishop of Ross pronounced the versicle of the Holy Spirit and the collect *Deus qui corda*. They spent the rest of this day in boundless merry-making and kept large bonfires burning in the streets and open spaces of the city while drinking wine in celebration. It was decided moreover to hold a solemn procession on the following Tuesday so as to celebrate the feast of the arrival of the privileges along with the feast of the arrival of the relics. Who can easily give an account of the character of that procession, the sweet-sounding praise of the clergy, the rejoicings of the people, the pealing of bells, the sounds of organs? On that day the prior celebrated a high mass of the Holy Spirit, the bishop of Ross preached a sermon to the clergy, and the beadle counted four hundred clergy besides lesser clerks and young monks taking part in this procession for the glory of God and the praise and honour of the [new] university, together with an astonishing crowd of people.

RODDY LUMSDEN

The Drop of a Hat

After some months of indecision,
Sykes decided to do his dissertation
on those events which actually had
occurred 'at the drop of a hat'.

He came across a minor skirmish
in the Netherlands War of Independence
caused when an insubordinate colonel
tossed a general's cap in the mud

and then discovered the 400 yards hurdles
at the 1904 St Louis Olympics
was started with the drop of a beret
when the starting gun had stuttered

but that was pretty much the limit,
his paper was returned, marked 'without merit'
though Sykes was later to fall for and marry
a girl who appeared as if from nowhere

and bumped him squarely into the gutter
while chasing her bonnet down Market Street.

Wages

from

Mr George Buchanan's opinion

anent

the reformation of the Universitie of St Andros.

The ordinar expensis of the college of humanitie.

Wagis of the personis

The principal ane hundreth pund.

The publik lectour ane hundreth markis.

The sex regentis sex scoir of pundis, to be diuidit at the principalis descretion, and paction maid with thayme.

The cuik and portar xij marks.

The steuart to be payit be the principal off the profet of the portionistis.

For colis, napre, veschel, and other extraordinaris concerning the hal and kitching xl pund yeirly.

For reparation of the place xl pund yeirly.

Of the quhilk reparation the principal sal geif coumpt yeirly to the censouris and rectour for the tyme.

ANNA CROWE

The Pier

an epithalamium for Mike and Sue

Built of squared, dressed sandstone, the pier
belongs to the land but ventures sturdily
along the line of the skerries, out to sea –
just far enough for its arm, bending at the elbow,
to fend off breakers from the small harbour.
In the channel the burn makes, flowing out
to meet the tide, two sycamore leaves are floating.
Below the bladder-wrack's rubbery frills
in the clear water bright green seaweed
lets its soft hair drift, this way
and that, stroking the sand.
Over the years, in spite of battering storms,
mussels and whelks have attached themselves
in bristling buttresses, and olive-green crabs
whose ancestors scuttled away
from the preaching of John Knox
shelter in crevices and cracks.
You can sit with the high wall at your back
in out-of-the-wind recesses – so snug,
a spider has spun some threads and caught four
white scraps of down. Two ochre stones below,
another has spread her web across the angle,
a two-inch doily dredged with grains of sand.

Small boats likes visiting friends tie up alongside,
casting a mooring over a weathered stanchion,
pocked and upright as a standing-stone
(a flight of slippery steps climbing mysteriously
from under the water). Most days, a cormorant
uses the breeze at the pier's end, perched on railings,

wings half-opened like a clerical umbrella.
At night a red lamp burns in passionate answer
to the Bell Rock's faithful pulsing on the horizon.
After a warm day the haar steals in,
bedewing railings, feathers, noses,
hanging with crystal drops the spider's web,
hiding the town and all its walls and towers.
Out on the pier you're in a white, vaporous room
where all you can see are the nearest waves,
those bales of grey-green silk unrolling
and flowing on like tireless music.

THOMAS A. CLARK

The Pier Walk

a few steps
will bring you out
into air and light

take it easy
don't hurry ahead
in anticipation

through a contrary
movement of water
you walk on stone

you are one alone
careless
yet having care

not to go
straight forward
but to be
straightforward

in a strict occasion
of shifting water
light and air

TOM POW

St Andrews

I am sitting in Pitigliano –
that human doocot, perched

on a spur of Tuscan rock –
thinking about St Andrews.

It's not so hard. February
in Tuscany's not how the pictures

play in your mind. I've seen
the charm of small-town piazzas

drabbed by a relentless
East coast rain and otherwise

delightful alleys so grey and cold
you'd think them splashed with salt.

But, this evening, the day turned
and, from the valley of the Meleta,

Pitigliano appeared to float
on its honeyed rock against

a properly azure sky.
In memory, once again, I saw

how St Andrews would likewise
stoke up all the clarity

an East coast day could offer,
till the town, miraculously, rose

on a bed of its very own golden
Tuscan light. At such times,

from within the warmth
of its evening walls, I'd hear

ringing out soundlessly –
over cornfields, turnip drills and sea –

the ghostly grey finger
of its ruined campanile.

RODDY LUMSDEN

The Designer's Dream

A featherie is sclatted off a wooden tee;
a gutty's rattled out of semi-rough;
a gourlay's pitched pin-high out of a bunker;
a *Titleist Distance* rolls into the cup.

These little white pills serve to send me under:
I watch a fairway spreading down a street;
a water hazard spills out of a sand dune,
the turf springs pleasingly beneath my feet.

Every night, it seems, the same thing happens:
moles and rabbits burrow through my dream.
And now, is this a woman's skin I'm touching,
or the skin-smooth surface of the perfect green?

ANDREW LANG

Ballade of the Royal Game of Golf
(East Fife)

There are laddies will drive ye a ba'
To the burn frae the farthermost tee;
But ye mauna think driving is a',
Ye may heel her, and send her ajee,
Ye may land in the sand or the sea;
And ye're dune, sir, ye're no worth a preen,

Tak' the word that an auld man'll gie,
Tak' aye tent to be up on the green!

The auld folk are crouse, and they craw
That their putting is pawky and slee;
In a bunker they're nae gude ava',
But to girn, and to gar the sand flee.
And a lassie can putt – ony she, –
Be she Maggy, or Bessie, or Jean;
But a cleek-shot's the billy for me,
Tak' aye tent to be up on the green!

I hae play'd in the frost and the thaw,
I hae play'd since the year thirty-three,
I hae play'd in the rain and the snaw,
And I trust I may play till I dee;
And I tell ye the truth and nae lee,
For I speak o' the thing I hae seen –
Tom Morris, I ken, will agree –
Tak' aye tent to be up on the green!

ENVOY

Prince, faith you're improving a wee,
And, Lord, man! they tell me you're keen;
Tak' the best o' advice that can be,
Tak' aye tent to be up on the green!

The Grip

Where I come from, the sky's much further away. But here – no joke – it's so flat I could put out my hand and touch it. And as the first train leaves Waverley I put my fingers to the window, like a kid. Later, over the rail bridge – the famous one – there's rain and then sun, and I count five seals sleeking the rocks at Burntisland, then a double rainbow, and I close my eyes – more of a wish than a prayer – and the weather picks up, or maybe I do and I lift my

I steady my

And I have to walk round the carriage, have to keep moving, just to stay loose; practise putting in the vestibule at the end of the train. That's what they say here – vestibule. Been dreaming shots for weeks, months, who knows how long. Dream other stuff too. Just last night – there was me and Arnie Palmer, and the Great White Shark and that bloke who lost his arm to a helicopter and Arnie says: 'I could never hit the ball hard enough to please him.'

The Shark steps up, turns his blond head before addressing the ball, 'Mate?'

'My old man,' says Arnie, and I can see he's cut up. The Shark nods, sympathetic, takes a swing, using the good arm of Helicopter as a club. He hits the ball far out on the Old Course, and it lands near the fourteenth hole, the place Tiger triumphed when he won the British Open – a blind shot lined up against a television crane.

And then it's my turn, but the Helicopter guy refuses his arm and I'm left with a four iron, swinging all over the shop, digging myself into the fairway. My swings are mad and short and nervous, the ball sits staring and all my weight is on the back foot.

Arnie turns and says: 'And you'll never please anyone, playing like that.'

* * *

Off at Leuchars. The day shifts, the sun's out and it's windy as hell. There's a hand-drawn sign on a whiteboard, outside the ticket office: 'Closed due to high winds.' Back home I'd been warned about the winds – they're the devil – anyone who's ever been here can tell you. There's a hand-written note on the door: 'Closed due to staff shortage'. Everything closed and the wind's up and I try not to look for omens. And then an almighty noise – bloody hell – a sonic boom, a racket like Concorde or something, and I make out two fighter jets. An American couple in front of me, and the woman looks up, nervous, *D'you think, to the war?* And her husband also looks up, grips her arm, *You betcha, to the war.* What I notice here, the war's a lot closer, that's for sure. And I notice, too, how I'm swearing these days, just inside, I mean, not out loud. At least, not if I can help it. My parents – God rest – never swore a day in their lives, wouldn't let a swear word through the front door. And there was that time Concorde flew over, way back – I was a young fella, just started in the office – and the noise of it and my mother, out into the back yard, wiping flour on her pinny – said the sound was like jets in the Second World War, the jets flying low – brownouts in Melbourne, she said – brown paper over the windows, to fool the Japanese.

Bloody hell, I'd looked up, following the sound.

Language, my mother frowned, and when my father got home she said: 'It flew over and you should've heard', here she rolled her eyes and looked at me, direct, the way only she could look.

'No need for that', said my father, putting his paper down. 'No need.'

They were old-fashioned, I guess you could say. Certain standards. And I was named after my father, people called us Old Bren and Young Bren, but you'd never call my father old to his face. Though they were pretty long in the tooth by the time I was born. An only child. They'd given up hope they said, and then I came along, bit of a miracle, by all accounts. And they were grateful. And we stayed close.

Anyway, that boom brings it all back and it's a busy train – and there's a few Japanese as a matter of fact – and then there's local boys – over-sized kids on under-sized bikes – leaping and roaring off the ramp leading to the bus, doing wheelies round the cases and the rucksacks and the men of a certain age. And it's only just gone eight and shouldn't these kids be at school? But I guess – August – their summer, our winter. My sense of time and season, it's all out of whack. Travelling does that to a person. Each of the men on the platform wears a cap, long shorts and socks with sandals. Then there's the v-neck. These men are my generation, I can see that. But I'm not with the cap or the jumper. As for the shorts. Arnie never did shorts, even if it was a hundred in the shade, no shorts, and I'm inclined to agree. One of the over-sized boys skids close on his bike, right up to my face, so close that his spots are in technicolour, 'Bloody yahoo,' I say, under my breath, and for a minute I think he's going to, seems he might, with the fists, and I grip the leather pouch round my waist, but he only spits and says, 'Fuck off grandpa.' Back home, I'd been warned about the language. The Scots, so they tell me, the Scots don't delete an expletive.

I'm not what you'd call a natural observer. But these past weeks with the travel, you're on high alert, all the time, to what's new and different and so far from your common or garden experience. Wary, too. What with the cheques and the cards and the passport. The travel pouch, I pat it every so often, just to make sure. And I notice everything, weighing it up – the weather, the food, the sky, the way people look. Saw a comedy show on TV the other night – they call it the telly here – and a Canadian comes on, been at the Festival: 'The Scotch', he says, 'The colour of them. They must sit in a basement, eating chalk.' It raised a laugh, though maybe not from the locals. Got me thinking. Blue-white, some of them, like the cream on the top of the milk we used to get at school. That milk, the way it curdled in the heat. Where I come from, no one is that colour, though we're careful about the sun, more careful than here by all accounts, what with the ozone and whathaveyou. Now it's all SPF60. Not like when I was a kid, marinated in baby oil and left to roast. *We know a lot more about some things and a lot less about others.* That's what Old Bren – God rest his soul – that's what he used to say.

And I'm here for him, that's the fact of it. And as we come into the town, adrenaline shoots through, and I have to move my fingers and toes, grip onto the seat in front, as if I were about to, as if I'm standing over. It's said that after retirement comes golf and after golf comes death, but it's clear a non-golfer first said that. And there's the Old Course Hotel and a patchwork of caps and sun on the shafts, and trees, and the sea beyond that, and it's green and rolling, greener than on TV, and bloody intimidating, if I'm to be honest, and golf's an honest man's game, if it's anyone's. And I miss my stop, what with all the excitement, and walk back to the clubhouse, dragging my suitcase on wheels, show my passport – booked well in advance and they tell me to pitch up tomorrow, early, before dawn, join the queue. From the clubhouse, I walk up to the Scores and I stand there awhile, breathing it all in, looking out over the sea – and it's the closest I've seen to beaches back home – none of these pebbles and whathaveyou. No. This is more like the Great Ocean Road. A bloody great sweep of sand.

I take out my pocket map. Turn right into North Street, looking for the B&B. It's still early and I'll be well in time for breakfast. Walk up towards the Cathedral – all part of my own private pilgrimage – past Johnston's of Elgin, and I repeat it to myself – the name so familiar. The Johnstons. The Scots family, up the street at home. Thirty years in the Parish, nine kids, same spelling – must tell them, must be some relation – past the golf shop with the sign: 'If you don't buy from us we both lose.' Open early. And on a whim, I go in and buy myself a new cap but the only loser is me – I tell you – parting with the cash here, travelling on the kangarouble – it's no joke – the cap over-priced, with a tick or a swoosh; then I walk past a tobacconist with a life-sized Red Indian out front (not sure if you can say that any more, Red Indian, but it's a bloody beauty, carved from red wood, something to do with cigars. And you'd not get away with that any more, not where I'm from). And I'm looking for number 121, and then I see it – a blue door, a sandstone plaque over the door on a grey stone building. It says: Old Tom Morris 1821–1908 born in a house which stood on this site, four time Open Champion, gives the dates. Tom Morris, a Giant of the Game, my father used to say. A hero. So I make a sign of the cross outside and keep walking up the road, past the cinema, past the place where that young Luther supporter was burned at the stake, the sort of carry-on, well, it has to be said – the sort of carry-on – let's face it – gives Catholics a bad name. Must remember and tell Father Dan. That's the thing about solo travel – always you're seeing things and wanting to tell someone after. Sometimes it gets to you. So I keep up the internal chat, as if there really was someone to tell. And I have to put it down on postcards as I go, just so I don't forget.

Past a small café – Episcopalian – and I pop in for some postcards – there's a bookshop attached and the smell of scones and tea and I promise I'll come back and treat myself tomorrow, after the game, and there's elderly ladies, very pleasant, older than me, behind the counter and a good selection of books, and I pick up one – *Johnny Cash's Spiritual Journey* – but put it down when I read about the death of his wife and his older brother. On the trip of a lifetime, some things are too sad to read about. And I look at the postcards and buy some of Market

Street and a few Celtic Benedictions, one for the Johnstons and for Father Dan and one for the Tierneys. There's a bell on the door and it tinkles as I go out and I continue on up to the ruins of the Cathedral and the sandstone arch at the end of the street. And it's unexpected, just how big it must've been, and I try not to think of the Luther supporter, simmering away, six hours it took, apparently. Some people take longer at the stake than others, that's just the way it is, taking body fat and size into consideration.

By this time, of course, I've walked too far, just enjoying myself, so I walk back a bit and find the B&B, though by the looks, it's more like one of those boutique hotels you read about. I've splashed out a bit here, though I'm not what you'd call naturally extravagant. My folks lived through the Depression, and I was brought up cautious with the pennies. But I got a good Super when I retired, and it's not every day – let's face it – not every day you come to the Home of Golf.

A lovely young woman opens the door and tells me she's the owner. Her and her husband, who's away just at the minute. They say that here – *just at the minute*. There's a fire in the grate, even though it's summer and golf memorabilia on all the walls, which suits me fine, and two large Buddha heads flanking the staircase, which strike me as odd, but it's kind of restful in here and she shows me round and here's the breakfast room, she says. And it's deep green on the walls, and an open fire and inwardly I groan because it's one long table and already there's a party of blokes – Irish, I think – tucking into the full shebang. I go upstairs and put my bags down, and then sit on the bed. I'm hungry, that's for sure, but, breakfast in these places. I dunno. I'm not what you'd call a morning person, never have been, and, for most of my life, it was never required.

Breakfast in our house, always the same. Toast, vegemite – real butter –

none of this margarine. Orange juice and cornflakes. Pots of tea, real tea with a strainer. With the folks – God rest – there was never any pass this, pass that, please and thank you – none of the palaver demanded of a person in the communal dining room. It's best when you have your own table, and don't have to pass anything, though there's always a little something in my experience (and how quickly I've chalked up experience) – a jug of milk here, a teaspoon there. And these breakfasts, you have to rearrange your morning face and make choices, for heaven's sake – soda bread, tattie scones, porridge; full English; full Scottish; bacon or no bacon; and most of it fried. Sometimes – no kidding – even the porridge smells fried. After six weeks on the road, I'm a connoisseur, as they say.

On that subject, my mother, she never fried a thing. Always watched the figure, always big on the home-cooked, the oven-baked. Kept my father and me on the straight and narrow, let me tell you, and one thing we'd never die of in our family – the lard. No way. But I look around these dining rooms these mornings, these last weeks, and the size of some of the – I've seen some whoppers, no kidding. Squeezed into all manner of tight-fitting, eye-popping whathaveyou. And some mornings, being a naturally retiring kind of bloke, it gets to be a bit much.

But I splash my face with water in the very white bathroom and then head downstairs, weary in my bones all of a sudden. And I pull up a pew next to the Irish boys, pro-golfers they tell me, and they pass the teapot (no strainer) and the landlady – Ailidh, her name is – comes to take my order. Apart from the Irish, there's a man and a woman, a couple, at the end of the table, over by the window – dressed in the Pringle and the check trousers – everything at least a size too small. And I'm thinking – golf? They couldn't walk to the. Not sure if they're American, to be fair, not all of them are. And I like to be fair. Golf's a game for a fair man.

And I smile and nod at the Irish boys and they're whingeing about the weather and how last night, they went looking for lap dancers, but couldn't find any. Imagine, they said, in a town this size?

Imagine, I agree, though to be honest, I'm not sure what they're on about. But the boys are good fun. Make me laugh. And I sit back, take it all in. Everything amuses me these days. But it wasn't always like this. I take after my mother. No sense of humour, she used to say. And she wasn't wrong. But Old Bren was different – a true life and soul. And I'm meeting some characters – let me tell you – these last six weeks. I tell this to the Irish boys. Half of Germany, three quarters of Sweden, they all seem to be on the road at once. They like to be here in August they tell me, because of the weather. I've met transsexual lovebirds and Italian skydivers. I've met a one-armed stuntman from Oregon. I've met an ex-Miss Croatia. Well, not exactly Croatia, but some place nearby. A bloody beauty, she was, really something. Travelling with her brother, though he didn't look like her brother. Anyway, all sorts. The kind you never get to meet in your regular life or at St Johns of a Sunday. And breakfast with these people, Good Morning, pass the, and so on. There's a whole world out there, at breakfast even, if you get my gist.

Anyway, the Irish boys ask where I'm from. And I tell him how the family is of Irish extraction – matter of fact – and I tell them about the trip. The Singapore stopover, the humidity – and Melbourne, Australia – that's right Mate, that's where I was born – and how the compression socks are a necessity, abso-bloody-lutely, for the long haul. I tell them about the hire car from Heathrow – always wanted to see Heathrow. Long before golf, I was interested in aviation. As a kid, wanted to be a pilot. And – what the hell was that racket at Leuchars? I remember to ask the landlady as she walks past. Bloody hell, for a minute there, so loud, thought it was Concorde. And the landlady laughs. Ailidh – I get her to spell her lovely name – though she hardly qualifies as a landlady – not the usual pillow bosom, ample hips – anyway, she tells us about the RAF base, the planes flying over. Not to the Middle East, not at the minute, but you never know, she shakes her head. You never know. 'We're all in it up to our bloody necks,' I say. And she shakes her head, but whether she's agreeing or not, it's hard to tell. Tower of London, and Buckingham Palace, I continue – not that I'm a fan of Betty Windsor – not by a long shot. Big Ben, London Bridge, the whole Monopoly board. How I took a red bus around the city. Did the same in Edinburgh and I'm impressed, I tell them. And the stories keep coming and they keep listening. And this is new, the telling of a story till the end. I keep expecting some interruption, someone to take up the slack, finish it for me. At home, it was always Old Bren with the stories. And when I'd start up, he'd finish, in his excitement, talk right over, as if I wasn't there. Not that I minded. Not at all. Not being one of life's natural raconteurs. But Old Bren, now, he could really spin a yarn. While I was always what you'd call shy. Never a one for the punchline. But here, people seem to like it, and I keep the stories rolling, just for the sheer enjoyment, it has to be said, the sheer bloody enjoyment of hearing my own voice, right through. And I scan their faces, every now and then, just to make sure, but the boys are all smiles and encouragement.

And what brings you here? Ailidh asks and I tell her it's the golf, but more than the golf. For my father, I say. Old Bren died a year ago – he was 89, a ripe old – you're not wrong there. And my mother died before him. Unusual, I know, for the wife to pre-decease, if that's the expression, and she never fried anything, not a thing, but it was the passive smoking. Old Bren (I've just started, just lately, calling him that), well, he was big on the baccy. Never did him any harm. For him, it was the dodgy ticker. Got him in the end. And it's a big thing, I tell her, to lose both parents in three months. Totally out of the blue. Knocked me for six, if I'm honest. And now, can you believe – I'm a 65 year old adult orphan? Imagine that, I say to her. And she flushes, and says she cannae imagine, as she leaves the room with the empty bowls, and I swear, she's so lovely, if I stay in this establishment one minute longer, I'll be head over the proverbial. No kidding. And I mention as much to the Irish boys who are all nudges and winks as they get up to leave, off to the Duke's today they tell me. Spain tomorrow. And I admit, I'm sorry to see them go.

Ailidh comes back in and I finish the story. Almost a year to the day, I tell her, since Old Bren died. And that's why I'm here. A pilgrimage, of sorts. I've been to Ireland, to Knock. Did the steps on my knees, which surprised me, because I've never been that kind of a believer. Been to Lourdes – the McDonalds of the sick. Really – don't even bother. After here, it's Italy. Il Papa. And I'm here, I tell her, because Old Bren liked a round or two, lived for the golf in fact, and he used to watch those people at Mass, at St Johns, our parish, people his own age, come back from their trips, come back from Scotland – always with the Pringle, parading up to Communion – and I wouldn't say he was jealous, Old Bren wasn't that kind of a fella, not by a long shot, but he was wistful. 'Tommy's been to the golf,' he'd say. 'Windy,' he tells me. 'The Old Course.' He'd shake his head. 'But the Scots didn't invent the game,' he'd say, 'they only invented the hole'. And some people'd make a meal out of that, some kind of innuendo, but not Old Bren. 'It'd be worth seeing, one day,' he'd say. 'The Old Course.'

And he would've liked to travel; I know that for a fact. But what with the dodgy ticker, and my mother, well, she developed, how do you say it – all the phobias, full blown – your claustro and your agora, you name it, she had it – and he didn't want to leave her. Devoted, that's the word. And I couldn't leave them. Nothing to do with the money. How many times did I offer to pay? And I could afford it, Victorian State Insurance, these past thirty-five years. General Manager. A good job. I miss it, course I do. Show me a man who doesn't miss his work, somewhere to go, a purpose, the tie and the suit. Show me a man who doesn't miss it and I'll show you a. That's where the golf comes in, and I never thought I'd hear myself say it. If you only live long enough, you hear yourself say lots of things. That's just a fact. Because my game was footy, for so many years, barracked for Carlton, the MCG box; the blazer, the works. Used to play too – but it's tough – Aussie Rules – all the high marks, it's a young man's game, make no mistake, and if you value your vertebrae, well. It's tough.

But old Bren's game was always golf. Took me out young, handed me the clubs, tried to instil the basics. Like Arnie Palmer's dad – the grip, the stance, the swing, the same advice: 'Hit it hard, go find it and hit it hard again.' But I never really took to it, until pretty recently, to tell you the truth. It was never really my game, went out occasionally, just to be social. But in the last year or so, what with my troubles, I'd go out on the driving range most days, a good place to think, or not think as the case may be, just for an hour or two, practise the putting, the driving, the chipping. Became kind of obsessed, to tell you the truth, at the local club, got the handicap down, now I'm a 13. Which isn't too bad, if I do say so myself.

And I'm on my second pot of tea and Ailidh's asking me in her soft voice: 'And what does your wife make of it, the golf?' And there's something in her expression when I tell her how I never married, no, and I see her working out the age of me, my neat appearance, and still living with the folks – recently deceased – and some kind of a question mark in her eyes – and it's not what you're thinking – I want to tell her. No question marks over my – how do you say it? – my so-called sexuality. Absolutely none whatsoever.

It's been a good life so far, I tell her, wife or no wife, and more to come, more life in the old dog, and maybe I should've met a girl such as herself twenty years ago. I say this out loud – I'm flirting, I realise this, a new sensation – and she seems to flirt back, and smiles, and so I confide that yes, there was a lady friend, once, years back, we stepped out for a while, and it was serious, but let's just say, Netta – my mother – didn't exactly go for her, and Old Bren wasn't too keen and that's just the way it was, back then. 'While you're under my roof,' and so on and so forth and I was young, and anyway, it's in the long ago, and this is a pilgrimage, did I mention that? 'Aye,' she says. She's got the dishes professionally stacked along one arm now, heading off to the kitchen, and she inclines her head to the window: 'Nice day for it.' And I look out and the wind's died right down. And I think how to fill in my time till tomorrow. And reluctant to leave her, I say, when she comes back, 'Would you mind? Just a tick?' And I spread my map and ask Ailidh as she removes the tablecloth, ask her to point out the Catholic Church, and I'm the last guest seated, and I can't seem to move, even though I should get in some sights, I know that.

'Aye,' she says, 'Just round the corner.'

And she turns away from me then with her soft accent and her soft eyes and her pale arms full of tablecloth and I've no more excuses.

'Thank you,' I say.

I go up to my room and check the lid and put the small urn in with my golf clubs, his old set. A travel urn. Who would've thought? A cremation, I know – unusual for a Catholic of his generation – but it was his wishes. Never wanted to be buried, all mouldering like that. Always partial to a barbie, he said.

* * *

The Church – it's small and sandstone and inside it's all marble – pure

Mediterranean, if you ask me, not that I've been there yet, to the Med – but the closer I get to the altar it seems that there's the shape of the Trinity, the outline of the three of them, but no substance to it, like a Turin shroud effect. And I wonder if it's been got at, must find out, must ask around. Maybe retaliation, for that poor burning boy, the one that barracked for Luther?

Fair's fair, I suppose. Fair enough.

And I light a candle this morning, for my good fortune. And for tomorrow. And I pray that I'll remember all the things I know. And when I get out there

I'll steady my

I'll lift my

And I focus on the candle flame. The white round centre of it. Genuflect, then with Holy water, cross myself three times, and then I'm out and heading down towards the Golf Museum, past the stained glass of the Royal and Ancient and a couple of R&A blokes, seated in the bay window, lift their glasses, first dram of the day. And I stand and watch a party at the tee off, near the white box, hold my breath, applaud along with the rest of them.

The golf museum. As I walk in, I pat the bronze shoulder of Old Tom Morris, the life size replica. I mooch my way round the exhibits – decide not to dress up as a 19th century golfer – but it's the last room that grabs me – all acid colours, greens and yellows and the names of different clubs on the wall. A room for kids. A happy room. It catches my eye. Kids. A sudden pang, just sometimes I have it, makes me wonder what it would've been like. Your own kids. A different life. Then out into the shop, think about souvenirs, a tea towel, a few postcards. Avoid the chocolate selection and the tins of mini boules – it's beyond me – why they'd be touting mini boules, and I give the furry animals a body swerve too and I'm just about to go out the glass door when I see it and have to double back: a row of bronze golfing hands in the window. Famous golfing grips and I'm in heaven, all of a sudden and I spend a good half hour examining this collection – donated by a keen golfer – the drummer from Bon Jovi, whatever that is. And they're all there – the Shark and Seve Ballesteros and Arnie. There's no Ben Hogan, but you can't have everything, and his grip was kind of singular. But there's something about Arnie's grip that gets me. What strikes me is the width of his wrists and fingers, and the look of them, like great shanks of meat. Nothing long or elegant about the hands. Just something huge and strong and unarguable about that grip. And I think about it long and hard and examine the hook of the little finger, the way he does it. And then I go outside and peer in at these rows of hands suspended above golf clubs that aren't there, floating in space. Something beautiful and godlike about it. Something that makes me want to bow my head and give thanks.

* * *

And then it's my turn. I'm lining up in the green v-neck, with the Old Course motif, and I can hear the congregation, the older ones, 'Young Bren's been away' they're saying, 'To the golf.' And Father Dan looks up, winks, and I want to tell him about the Luther boy, and young Ailidh, and the Red Indian with the cigars and I take the wafer on the tongue in the old way, and as he raises it in front of me, something about the shape of it, and the colour, and I'm off, back there, following the ball after it's been hit, can still see the image of it. Body of Christ, I repeat, the wafer dissolving. 'Young Bren's been away,' and soon, Mass'll be over, and I'll be telling how it was, no interruptions, we'll be sitting there in the Presbytery, my glass raised and the bottle well open. The full story. About the Church and the wind and the five holes of rain, all of it, and how I stood there, with the knees bent, full focus – didn't want to make a fool – and the pressure of the crowds round the clubhouse, and how I felt as if he was there, as the wind started up, as if the Old Bastard, up in Heaven – I'm pretty sure about Heaven – as if he was putting me off my stroke, and it's a major thing, I know, cursing the dead, but my arms were lead weight, dead weight all of a sudden, and who really knows the meaning of the words till they've shouldered a coffin? And how I kept putting it off, spreading him to the Old Course, even though I knew that's what he wanted.

How my luck held until the fourteenth, where I'd driven off the tee, a pure long shot, 280 yards, went for the green, decided to slice it, avoid Hell bunker, but that's where I end up, with a three wood it takes me two shots to get out, I'm left forty yards from the pin and it all goes horribly wrong, but then, by the eighteenth, it's magic, even the caddie is impressed, and it's all over way too soon, and how I stopped on the bridge to wave, like the Legends, like you do – how I got the photo to prove it – my own golf story, the ashes in my pocket and Arnie's voice in my head.

DOUGLAS DUNN

A St Andrews Garden

from *'Body Echoes'*

Against the sounds of the sea, a roof-top dove
Performs its throated wooing. Much bird-song,
Chirping courtships, this twenty-fourth of March
By a window where a St Andrews garden
Shows off a bright azalea and a palm
In a Himalayan boast crossed with hot
Tropical green, a girl shaking her hands
At a sink. It has very deep sweetness,
This moment, colossal sugar, brilliant
Ambrosial light, and I almost forget
The woman I saw earlier today
From Innes's corner, crossing South Street,
When time wrinkled and the cars changed, years
Unwound themselves in a reversed photoflood.
I had no name to call. I saw a sound
And neither eye nor ear could hold it.

WALTER SCOTT

Carved in Runic Characters

16 SATURDAY 1827 The ruins at St Andrews have been lately cleared out. They had been chiefly magnificent from their size not their extent of ornament. I did not go up to Saint Rule's tower as on former occasions; this a falling off for when before did I remain sitting below when there was a steeple to be ascended? But the Rheumatism has begun to change that vein for some time past though I think this is the first decided sign of acquiescence in my lot. I sate down on a gravestone and recollected the first visit I made to St Andrews now 34 years ago. What changes in my feeling and my fortune have since then taken place, some for the better, many for the worse. I remembered the name I then carved in runic characters on the turf beside the castle gate and I asked why it should still agitate my heart.* But my friends came down from their tower and the foolish idea was chased away.

* The name was that of Williamina Belsches, to whom Scott had proposed in 1795. She turned him down.

After Many Days

The mist hangs round the College tower,
           The ghostly street
Is silent at this midnight hour,
           Save for my feet.

With none to see and none to hear,
           Downward I go
To where, beside the rugged pier,
           The sea sings low.

It sings a tune well loved and known
           In days gone by,
When often here, and not alone,
           I watched the sky.

That was a barren time at best,
           Its fruits were few;
But fruits and flowers had keener zest
           And fresher hue.

Life has not since been wholly vain,
           And now I bear
Of wisdom plucked from joy and pain
           Some slender share.

But, howsoever rich the store,
           I'd lay it down,
To feel upon my back once more
           The old red gown.

LINDA GREGERSON

Half Light

(George Wishart)

1.

The broad way and the narrow, you see, in
                    Upper
            Paleozoic shale, the argument having

come to this. If one side – call it *mine* – sets
                    forth
            the virtues of method and rich

supply and, not so incidentally, of Rome and all
                    its heirs,
            the other – *countermine* – shows

what a pickaxe and shovel can do with
                    only the
            sound of the enemy's digging to

guide them. Vernacular testament, tables
                    of stone. And
            here where the two converge and as

a consequence where many died the
                    siege
            returned to stalemate. I shall never

think of *undermine* as merely of the mind
                    again.

2.

Because the man would not keep

still, would preach against the errors of the
                    Church in
            Leith, in Montrose, wherever abatement

of the plague allowed. And furthermore
                    taught
            New Testament Greek. Was burned

at the stake on the first of March in 1546, you
                    may stand
            on the spot: unparalleled

view of northern coastline, sea, more rock.
                    The Cardinal
            said to have watched from the window where later

('a butcher') his body was hung. So two
                    to begin with: one
            in flames, the other unburied for seven

months, two versions of the one idea. Wishart's
                    friends, 'the first
            reformed congregation in Scotland,' held

the castle for nearly a year, their countermine
                    having saved
            the walls. The sea? Quite faithless. Would not

take sides. Indifferent to bombardment as to
                    filth
          from the privies of righteousness, which

emptied on the cliffs below. The English
                    reinforcements so
          long looked-for (this will not

surprise you) did not come.

                    3.

                    You've got
          to be ready, my gardener said just moments

before his sod cutter severed the cable line.
                    Referring not
          to lines so easily spliced but to his brother's

death at fifty, thus his own ('the family
                    heart').
          Nor did he mean this loveliness is lost

on him: I've seen him with the lilies and
                    the weeping
          larch. And look, he'll say. The motion

that begins among the crowns of oak and maple well
                    before it turns
          to weather on the ground, he means, whereas

I'm lost unless the front has warranted
        some mention
           on the morning news. So second- or third-

hand, much as I've always lived on the earth. The
        difference
           is not nature – my gardener loves

his new machines – but something more elusive
        yet, some
           lightness of touch that by a common

paradox bespeaks the firmer grasp.
        George
        Wishart in St Andrews would approve.

4.

I think he would. The lurid
        light
        of martyrdom was always in this sense

an aberration, like the mounting of cannon atop
        a church. The
        church in question (1546 again) has

largely gone to grass and bare foundation stone,
        the choir
        and transepts unimpeded green. Which leaves

the quarrel where exactly? If the wall
                that held
        a window (fallen churches turn to open

excavations for the enterprising urban poor)
                has been removed
        to bolster up a cowshed here, a roadwork farther

west of town, in what sense can the window
                still be said
        to govern point of view? Nostalgia? Backward

longing not so much for death-by-proxy as
                for that
        which makes the dying incidental. Hence

our beggarly rapture at stark divides: the cliffs
                on one side, North
        Sea on the other, and the mutilated

body (there is nothing quite so good at this)
                for scale.

George Wishart (1513–1546), schoolmaster, preacher, Protestant martyr, was condemned for heresy and burned at the stake in the earliest years of the Scottish Reformation. His sermons are said to have converted John Knox. Cardinal David Beaton (1494–1546), Archbishop of St. Andrews, presided over the death of Wishart and was murdered in turn by a group of Wishart's followers, who proceeded to occupy the Archbishop's residence. The subterranean passage (the mine) dug by Catholic forces during the siege that followed was intended to cause the collapse of the castle walls. The subterranean passage dug by Protestant defenders from inside the castle (the countermine) foiled the attack. The castle fell in June of 1547, after French ships arrived to join the bombardment. Surviving defenders, including John Knox, were turned over to the French as galley slaves. *L.G.*

Reformation

Upon the penult day of June [1547], appeared in the sight of the Castle of Saint Andrews twenty-one French galleys, with a skeife [division of] an army, the like whereof was never seen in that Firth before. ... The next day, after that the galleys arrived, they summoned the house, which being denied, (because they knew them no magistrates in Scotland), they prepared for siege. And first they began to assault by sea, and shot two days. But thereof they neither got advantage nor honour; for they danged the slates off houses, but neither slew man, nor did harm to any wall. But the Castle handled them so, that Sancta Barbara (the gunners' goddess) helped them nothing; for they lost many of their rowers, men chained in the galleys, and some soldiers, both by sea and land. And further, a galley that approached nigher than the rest was so dung with the cannon and other ordnance that she was stopped under water and so almost drowned, and so had been, were it not that the rest gave her succour in time, and drew her first to the west sands, without the shot of the Castle, and thereafter to Dundee, where they remained, till that the Governor, who then was at the siege of Langhope, came unto them, with the rest of the French faction. The siege by land was confirmed about the Castle of Saint Andrews, the xxiiij day of July. The trenches were cast; ordnance was planted upon the Abbey Kirk, and upon Saint Salvator's College (and yet was the steeple thereof burnt), which so annoyed the Castle, that neither could they keep their block-houses, the Sea-tower head, nor the west wall; for in all these places were men slain by great ordnance. Yea, they mounted the ordnance so high upon the Abbey Kirk, that they might discover the ground of the close in divers places. Moreover, within the Castle was the pest [plague] (and divers therein died), which more effrayed some that was therein, than did the external force without. But John Knox was of another judgment, for he ever said, 'That their corrupt life could not escape punishment of God'; and that was his continual advertisement, from the time that he was called to preach. When they triumphed of their victory (the first twenty days they had many prosperous chances) he lamented, and ever said, 'They saw not what he saw.' When they bragged of the force and thickness of their walls, he said, 'They should be but egg-shells.' When they vaunted, 'England will rescue us,' he said, 'Ye shall not see them; but ye shall be delivered in your enemy's hands, and shall be carried to a strange country.'

Upon the penult of July at night, was the ordnance planted for the battery; xiiij cannons, whereof four were cannons royal, called double cannons, besides other pieces. The battery began at four hours in the morning, and before ten hours of the day, the whole south quarter, betwix the fore-tower and the east block-house, was made assaultable. The lower transe was condemned, divers slain in it, and the east block-house was shot off from the rest of the place. Betwix ten hours and eleven, there fell a shower of rain, that continued near an hour, the like whereof had seldom been seen. It was so vehement, that no man might abide without a house. The cannons were left alone. Some within the Castle were of judgment, that men should have issued [forth] and put all in the hands of God. But because that William Kirkcaldy was communing with the Prior of Capua, who had the commission of that journey from the King of France, nothing was enterprised. And so was appointment made, and the Castle [sur]rendered, upon Saturday, the last of July.

RUDYARD KIPLING

A Rector's Memory

(St Andrews, 1923)

The Gods that are wiser than Learning
  But kinder than Life have made sure
No mortal may boast in the morning
  That even will find him secure.
With naught for fresh faith or new trial,
  With little unsoiled or unsold,
Can the shadow go back on the dial,
  Or a new world be given for the old?
    But he knows not what time shall awaken,
     As he knows not what tide shall lay bare,
    The heart of a man to be taken –
     Taken and changed unaware.

He shall see as he tenders his vows
  The far, guarded City arise –
The power of the North 'twixt Her brows –
  The steel of the North in Her eyes;
The sheer hosts of Heaven above –
  The grey warlock Ocean beside;
And shall feel the full centuries move
  To Her purpose and pride.
Though a stranger shall he understand,
  As though it were old in his blood,
The lives that caught fire 'neath Her hand –
  The fires that were tamed to Her mood.
And the roar of the wind shall refashion,
  And the wind-driven torches recall,
The passing of Time and the passion
  Of Youth over all!

And, by virtue of magic unspoken
  (What need She should utter Her power?)
The frost at his heart shall be broken
  And his spirit be changed in that hour –
    Changed and renewed in that hour!

Taking Stock

Betsy Sutherland slammed the gear into reverse, and glared at the small rectangle of sea in her mirror. What was it the woman had said? She looked down at her notebook on the passenger seat beside her and tried to decipher her notes. Go straight on past the harbour, she read, awkwardly craning her neck, then turn left into the field when you get to the gate. She turned the car round and drove past a forlorn row of houses until she came to an open metal gate. Swinging the car to the left she changed into second and set off down the muddy track.

'Blast!' Betsy put her foot down hard on the accelerator only to feel the car sticking in the mud. She must stop doing this, she thought, as she eased into first, after all this was hardly a front-page story. She must learn to delegate things better. She still needed to sort that Spanish piece, and heaven knows when she would get to her staffing appraisal. What was the point of being the boss if she couldn't cherry-pick her assignments?

Suddenly the sea was ahead of her. She stared at its glassy surface and shivered. She had never been able to understand people's fascination with the sea. Oh it was all very well on a sunny day, but then how many sunny days could you realistically expect in the East Neuk of Fife? Given the choice, she'd plump for a heated swimming pool every time. Not that she'd had the choice very often, she reflected, as she turned the car along the track so that she was parallel with the sea, in fact she found it hard to remember the last time she'd been away. There was that disastrous weekend in London Brenda had organised for her fortieth – but she preferred not to think about that. No, if she was honest, the last time she'd had a proper holiday, a holiday away in a hotel with sun and a swimming pool, was with Greg.

How much further could it be? She opened the window an inch and felt the chill sea air on her face. Thinking about Greg made her irritable, particularly since it reminded her she was due to meet yet another of the 'matches' picked for her by 'The Executive Dating Agency' that evening. She was beginning to wonder whether she shouldn't just phone and call the interview off when she saw the caravan ahead of her.

It was a dismal enough place to live. Perched on the edge of the cliff with its back to the sea, it looked from this distance like a plastic toy dropped by a careless child. On either side were the remains of a cabbage field, the stalks picked over by a few grubby sheep. Betsy glanced at her notebook and tried to remember what Mrs Gould had said on the phone. Was it forty years they had been here? She slowed the car to avoid a sheep that had strayed onto the track and tried to imagine what it must be like to be stuck up here in the middle of winter.

What was that she could see in front of the caravan? Something white was flapping in the breeze like a flag. As she drew closer she realised a line of washing had been strung between two poles and that what she had thought was a flag was in fact a sheet. That was something else she must talk to Simon about. For now that she came to think of it she wasn't at all sure that Simon knew how to use the washing machine. Oh he'd been in the kitchen when she'd set it going often enough, he may even have stuffed his dirty clothes into the drum, but as with so many other things she was beginning to realise now that he was actually leaving home she doubted whether he had ever done it for himself. She made a mental note to show him which setting and how much powder to use when she got in. It wouldn't do for him not to know how to wash his clothes now that he was going to university.

She was quite close now. On one side of the caravan was a neat trellis with some kind of evergreen growing up it. Daffodils were flowering in pots round the door. There was a paved area in front of the caravan edged with shells. She found a place to park and collected her papers from the front seat.

'Mrs Gould?' The woman who opened the door looked younger than she had expected.

'I'm Betsy Sutherland. From *The Gazette*.'

The first thing that struck Betsy as she stepped inside the caravan was how small it was. Straight ahead of her was a settee which she suspected must also serve as the Goulds' bed, to her right a sink and draining-board, and to her left a fold-down table. Above the settee was a curtained window framing a view of the sea. Every available inch of wallspace was used for storage.

She sat on a folding chair opposite the Goulds. With their permission she took out her tape-recorder and set it going. Then she flicked open her notebook and began her questions. It was Mrs Gould who spoke first.

'We came here in the summer of '62. We hadn't long been married. It was our first holiday. It was a proper site then, with a toilet block and showers and a shop and everything. There must have been a hundred caravans. The weather was glorious. I'd never lived so close to the sea before. We used to walk for miles right along the sand, sometimes as far as St Andrews. In the evenings people got together – there were parties down at the harbour. Dave loved to talk to the fishermen. His father was in the navy and he'd always longed to be near the sea. One day he went out on a catch and that was it really. We couldn't see any point in going back to Glasgow.'

Betsy typed the full stop and clicked off her tape-recorder. She reached for the glass of water she always kept on her desk and took a sip. In the end she'd had a productive afternoon. She'd established that the plot of land on which the Goulds had their caravan was to be sold off by the Council and that a planning application had been submitted for thirty-five houses. She hadn't got very far with the Planning Department but someone she knew on the Council who owed her a few favours had agreed to do some digging. Prices in the East Neuk had shot up over the past twelve months and if permission went through for a new development someone stood to make a fortune. She was beginning to smell a story. She wound the tape forward. She wanted to quote Mrs Gould talking about the state of repair of the caravan. Yes, this was the place.

' . . . I suppose it is a bit of an eyesore. We've thought about repainting

it – the rust has got a lot worse these past couple of years – but Dave isn't really up to it. The window could do with replacing too. When it rains I have to wedge tea-towels round the edge to stop the water coming in. We did manage to get the trellis repaired last winter and thank goodness the honeysuckle survives the salt. I dare say it's shielded a bit by the caravan.'

Betsy suddenly became aware of the phone ringing on her desk. She picked it up. A voice she didn't recognise asked to speak to her. She replied cautiously, surprised that an unknown caller should have got through to her direct line, when it dawned on her who it was. She glanced at the clock on the wall opposite then down at her diary. Yes, there it was, Gallagher's coffee shop, five-thirty. Her 'executive date' had completely slipped her mind. She apologised as well as she could but she could tell her would-be match was unimpressed. She sighed as she let him hang up.

The interruption reminded her of another promise. She had told Simon she would be back by seven and that she would make dinner for his last evening. It was now twenty past six and she still hadn't drafted out her piece. She would need another hour, especially as she was taking the next day off to drive Simon down to York. She dialled the number and listened to her own voice on the answering machine. When the beep came she left a message.

'Hello darling, listen, if you're there can you pick up the phone?' Betsy waited for a moment, watching the second-hand tick round on the clock. 'I'm afraid I'm going to be later than I said. There's something I have to finish off here. I promise I'll be back by eight and I'll pick up a take-away for us on the way. In the meantime if you're hungry there's plenty of pie left in the fridge. Just help yourself.'

She clicked the phone dead. She felt bad about the call. She stared at a photograph of Simon aged about four on her desk. There was hardly anything left of the blond, dimpled boy who held out his arms to her hoping she would pick him up. She took off her glasses and rubbed her forehead. She had never meant for it to be like this. As a young woman she had always imagined having lots of children. If, aged twenty, she had been asked to paint a picture of how she wanted her life to be she would have drawn herself in the kitchen, baking cakes while helping an assortment of rosy-faced children make animals from coloured card. When Simon was born Greg was still taking his exams so there'd been no choice but for her to go back to work. At the time she hadn't minded too much because she was good at her job and she'd thought that once Greg qualified and the next baby came she could stop. But the next baby hadn't come, Greg had left and she'd risen swiftly through the ranks of the paper until she was chief editor. She had always meant to spend more time with Simon, always hoped that she might remarry, but somehow things got in the way. There never seemed to be time to stop and take stock. Tomorrow she was driving Simon to York University for his 'Freshers' Weekend' and when he came back again at Christmas he would be a visitor.

Well if it was too late for her, she was damn well going to make sure it wasn't too late for the Goulds! She woke up her lap-top and started typing. Phrases formed in her mind. 'Forty years of shocking neglect.' That should make a few heads turn. 'Council drag heels on forgotten couple after developer's bribe.' If she could get away with a headline like that, she might even print it on the front page. At the very least her piece would put pressure on the Council to find the Goulds somewhere decent to live. The more she wrote the more scandalous it appeared to her. The Goulds had spent the better part of their lives in that box. It was almost a prison sentence. Just because they weren't the sort to make a fuss didn't mean they didn't deserve better treatment. Within an hour, Betsy had a story that should ensure the Goulds went straight to the top of the Council housing list.

As Betsy drove out of the car park she checked her watch. It was later than she had meant it to be. Still, if she put her foot down she would be home before nine and she and Simon could salvage what was left of the evening. She'd pick up some beers at the off-licence next to the take-away. She didn't much care for beer herself but Simon was increasingly scathing about her liking for white wine. She turned off the High Street and passed the church. On the right was Simon's first school. It scarcely seemed a moment since she had led him into the hall to join all the other new children waiting nervously with their parents. Even now she could not admit to herself how much she was going to miss him.

Her thoughts drifted back to the night Greg left. With hindsight she supposed she should have seen it coming. If she was honest there had been plenty of warning signs – late appointments, sudden weekends away – but she suspected the real truth was that she had been too busy coping with her job, the house, Simon, to notice. She remembered the date, the 17th of June. Greg had phoned to say he was going to be late. She had taken the call in the sitting room, staring at the Bonnard poster Brenda had given her. Greg's diary was open on his desk and there was a heart drawn in the top right-hand corner of the page. It was only a tiny heart but it was so unexpected amongst the lists of clients and meetings that it had caught her attention. She had stared at the heart trying to think what it could mean. It wasn't Valentine's day or their wedding anniversary or any other special day she could think of. Next to the heart was what looked like a phone number. She had puzzled over this as she went back into the kitchen. She cleared away supper, gave Simon his bath and got him into bed, and then settled down to her own work. Still the truth did not dawn on her. As it grew late her ears strained for the sound of Greg's car in the drive. She began to argue with herself, remembering an accident she had read about in the paper in which a man had been killed driving home from work. When midnight came she went back into the sitting room and dialled the number. 'Hi,' a voice sang out at her from an answering machine, 'you're through to Natasha. I can't take your call right now but if you leave your name and number I'll get back to you.'

Betsy swung the car into her drive and switched off the engine. It was only then that she remembered the take-away. For a moment she wondered whether she should turn the car round and go back for it, but she quickly decided against it. She was late enough as it was. She had some rice in the deep-freeze, and she could easily rustle up a stir-fry. She'd put in plenty of soy sauce, the way Simon liked it. She'd forgotten the beer too, but there was a bottle of single malt in the cupboard she'd been saving for a special occasion. They could open that.

She let herself in through the front door. The lights were on. She took off her coat and carried her bag into the kitchen. On the cooker was a pan of baked beans, still slightly warm. Next to the sink was a freshly washed plate and a small heap of cutlery. She couldn't help smiling to herself. Simon was learning. She turned to the fridge and saw a note pinned behind a magnet. 'Gone to meet Chris', she read, 'have eaten. Back late. Love Simon.' She took the note and sat down with it at the table. She was angry with herself now. Even on Simon's last night she had managed to blow it. Still, she reasoned, as she poured herself a glass of her favourite Chardonnay, she would have him all day tomorrow. It would take at least six hours to drive to York, and she'd already made enquiries about where they might stop for lunch. Chris was Simon's best friend and off to Warwick University and she could see that they might want to spend their final evening together. She opened the fridge and took out an apple and some cheese. It was hardly worth making a stir-fry just for herself. She put the apple, cheese and her glass of wine on a tray and carried it into the sitting room. She kicked off her shoes and stretched her legs out on the sofa, feeling her muscles relax. She'd just lie here in the quiet for a few moments and relish the peace. Later she could run a hot bath, perhaps have a look at a film. Simon wouldn't be back for hours and they didn't need to leave early in the morning. She reached her hand out for her glass and took a sip of her wine.

Snippets of the day floated in and out of her mind. She didn't try to stop them. She thought of the neat arrangement of cupboards inside the Goulds' caravan, the extraordinary vista of sea from their window. It must be a bit like living on a ship. She could imagine how beautiful it would be up there in the summer, with the waves breaking round the rocks on the shore below. It would be a wrench to the Goulds to have to leave. They would hardly be able to afford one of the new houses that would be built on the land. It was all very well for the Council to decide that the Goulds needed moving on, but what if they didn't want to leave, what if they preferred to stay in their caravan? She hadn't thought to ask them that. As Betsy settled back against the cushions her story took on a new shape. It was the Goulds' home after all, she pondered, taking another sip of her wine and savouring its rich honey flavours. And apart from the repairs that needed doing they had seemed perfectly happy with their lot. She contemplated the Bonnard poster she had hung above the fireplace. Greg had hated its clutter of objects, the slovenly posture of the woman at the table, but she could look at it for hours. She let her mind loose in the glorious colours. She'd make a fresh appointment with the Goulds and go and see them first thing on Monday morning, she decided. She'd book a photographer and try and get some shots. They could take the Goulds standing in front of their caravan with the panorama of sea behind. The pots of daffodils should add a nice touch. If they had a sunny weekend, who knows, perhaps the honeysuckle would be in bloom.

KATHLEEN JAMIE

The Puddle

St Andrews

A week's worth of rain
musters in play-parks;
pools in hollow
low-lying fields

signal come-hither
to oystercatchers; curlews
insert like thermometers
their elegant bills.

What is it to lie so
level with the world,
to encourage the eye
-for-the-main-chance

black-headed gulls,
goal-posts, willows,
purple-bellied clouds
to inhabit us, briefly

upside down? Is it written
that we with a few
years left, God willing,
must stake our souls

upright within us
as the grey-hackled heron
by a pond's rim,
constantly forbidding

the setting winter sun
to scald us beautifully,
ruby and carnelion?
Flooded fields, all pulling

the same lustrous trick,
that flush in the world's light
as though with sudden love –
how should we live?

Construction for a Site: Library on an Old Croquet Lawn, St Andrews. Nine Approaches

1.

Step down
into the silence, a green
pool.

2.

Forget
the sea is here.
From where you are
you cannot see
the sea.
Stop your ears.

3.

Swim
the length of this empty
pool, slowly.
Turn, anchor yourself dead centre.
Measure yourself one minute
against four green walls,
the domestic slant of the kitchen garden,
the perfectly right-
angled clipped box-hedge
and you're sunk.

4.

On the old croquet lawn
blackbird bounces
at his killing game.
On the site of the new library
accurate blackbird extracts
fat facts of worms.
Wink
back at him, he'll
zig off waggling
the tail-end of an idea.

5.

Listen,
chilly birdsong
sprinkling icewater
over the garden, a tap
turning on and off again.
Library silence.

6.

This is the lie of the land.
This is the house.
This is the staggered line of trees, Maytime
still struggling to bloom in a seawind,
daisies snatching shut-eye in the shade,
bluebells bruising blue, the late

late primroses on the cold slope.
This is the ironwork of the old gate.
It does not open.
It does not remind you of a prison.
This is the garden laid out for a gentle game
and when the garden grows
this is the wall that shelters.
This is the cutout crowstepped arch
that frames the savage castle.
Don't
let history frame you
in a pretty lie.

7.

When
imaginary Alice in flimsy
muslin shivers slightly in
a heatwave in Nineteen Ten and
Hugh does a handstand on the barbered grass hurrahs
as Frederick's mallet chips
a perfect one through oh refuse
to pretend to remember
the flavour of those
last of the raspberries that
Rab (cap-off) the gardener's
boy brought over (and which he did not taste).
Refuse to pretend to remember
how he and very decorated Frederick would both
be fattening worms in France
not six years later.

Freeze them in sepia.
Refuse to pretend to remember.

8.

the garden as mirror of man's logical scientific
        and ordered mind.
the library as garden.
the library as mirror of man's logical scientific
        and ordered mind.
the garden as game.
the garden as mirror of man's logical scientific
        and ordered mind.
the game as mirror.
the mind as mirror of man's logical scientific
        and ordered garden.
the library as game.
play the garden.

9.

The Formal Garden
(as the mind in the library) turns
in on itself. Croquet
and contemplation put us
through hoops. Consider.

The Corner of Abbey Street and Greenside Place

for AHR

He was my friend and I listened when he told me
things I had never wanted to hear. And I said nothing
which was all he wanted me to say.

We drank from a bottle of wine until it was empty
and the gas-fire ran out its shilling. Then we went outside
and walked together in the wind.

Some silence grew in the middle of his words (he
never stopped talking), some silence we would never need to break,
some things we need never mention again. On the corner,

when we stopped outside the windows of their house,
the windows were dark. All these people we both loved so hopelessly,
behind their windows they all were sleeping.

The Rush of the Aurora Borealis

A thoroughly congenial and indeed brilliant little society, St Andrews has become too well known to demand much description. Its fame, which is partly of letters, but I fear still more of golf, has extended far and wide, and there are now few places where the visitor is more likely to meet with other pilgrims from all quarters of the world. The little grey town with its rocks and ruins, the stately relics of a historico-ecclesiastical period now entirely passed, and leaving no sign except in these monuments of a lodging far more magnificent than faith or learning has ever since had in Scotland, – with the dark and dangerous reefs below, which make St Andrews Bay a name of fear to seafaring men; and around the half-encompassing sea, sometimes grey as northern skies can make it, sometimes crisp and brilliant in its blue breadth, as full of colour as the Mediterranean; the long stretch of sandhills and cheerful links, the brown and red roofs all clustered about an old steeple or two, thinning out into farmhouses and cottages land-ward among their spare and wind-swept trees, running down into fisher-houses, and the bustle of a little storm-beaten port towards the east, – stands now, as then, upon its little promontory, with all those charms of situation and association which make a place of human habitation most dear. I think there is no such sweep and breadth of sky anywhere. The 'spacious firmament on high' sweeps round and round, with the distant hills in soft outline against its tints of pearl, and the levels of the sea melting into it, yet keeping their imperceptible line of distinction, brimming over in that vast and glorious cup. The great globe sways visibly in the summer sunshine, so that the musing spectator seems to see its vast circumference, the level of its human diameter, the circle that holds it separate from all other spaces and worlds. Nowhere else has my mind received the same impression of the round world and all that it contains. And there could be no more magnificent sight anywhere than the sunsets that flame upon the western sky over the long levels of the links, or the rush of the aurora borealis in the intense blue of the midnight frost, or the infinite soft gradations of earth and sea and air in the lingering summer evenings, when the gleam of half-a-dozen lighthouses comes out intermittent, like faint earthly stars in the dim celestial circles when silence reigns and peace.

J. M. BARRIE

from *Courage*
The Rectorial Address Delivered at St Andrews University May 3rd 1922 to the Red Gowns of St Andrews

... spirits walk.

They must sometimes walk St Andrews. I do not mean the ghosts of queens or prelates, but one that keeps step, as soft as snow, with some poor student. He sometimes catches sight of it. That is why his fellows can never quite touch him, their best beloved; he half knows something of which they know nothing – the secret that is hidden in the face of the Mona Lisa. As I see him, life is so beautiful to him that its proportions are monstrous. Perhaps his childhood may have been overfull of gladness; they don't like that. If the seekers were kind he is the one for whom the flags of his college would fly one day. But the seeker I am thinking of is unfriendly, and so our student is 'the lad that will never be old'.

A Memory

Fickle of choice is Memory
But, hidden within her secret deeps
She guards whate'er in life may be
Vivid and sweet perpetually,
And of the loved strict treasury keeps.

There childhood's flowers bloom for aye,
There in a quiet, grave, profound,
Those whom dark death has lured away
Live on, with peace unchanging crowned,
Immune from ageing time's decay.

Keeps she for me, then, safe-enshrined –
Cold of the north – those bleached grey streets;
Grey skies, a glinting sun, a wind
From climes where sea with ocean meets;
And ruinous walls by tempests pined.

There history in romance doth hide:
Martyr and saint, Pict, Scot, Culdees:
They dared, fought, suffered, dreamed and died,
Yet of their long wild centuries
Left but these stones their bones beside.

Ghosts in that sunlight come and go:
Columba, David, Margaret,
Bothwell the fierce, dark Rizzio,
And she, caught fast in fate's fell net,
Mary, the twice-queened, fair as snow.

The happy daylight wanes, the tide
Lays a cold wreath of foam upon
Its sea-worn rocks, the billows ride
In endless cavalcade — are gone:
The rose of eve burns far and wide.

Hedge School

Not only those rainy mornings our great-great-grandmother was posted at
a gate
with a rush mat
over her shoulders, a mat that flashed
Papish like a heliograph, but those rainy mornings when my daughter and
the rest

of her all-American Latin class may yet be forced to conjugate
Guantanamo, amas, amat
and learn with Luciana how 'headstrong liberty is lash'd
with woe' – all past and future mornings were impressed

on me just now, dear sis,
as I sheltered in a doorway on Church Street in St Andrews
(where, in 673, another Maelduin was bishop),

and tried to come up with a ruse
for unsealing the *New Shorter Oxford English Dictionary* back in that corner
shop
and tracing the root of *metastasis.*

ROBERT CRAWFORD

St Andrews

I love how it comes right out of the blue
North Sea edge, sunstruck with oystercatchers.
A bullseye centred at the outer reaches,
A haar of kirks, one inch in front of beyond.

ROBIN ROBERTSON

Mayday 1997

The tide's twist,
its rack and pinion,

is paying out
black chains of water

into St Andrew's bay:
the scuttle of the wave

redistributes the pebbles,
putting the beach in a new pattern.

Sunlight is prinkling
the sliding sea

till the wind lifts
and riffles the surface to silver:

the scales of some axle-fish
turning to bask.

Aig Fèis Bàrdachd Cill Rìmhinn

Bha mi air mo dhòigh am bàrd fhaicinn
ach cha chuala mi gu ceart e
leis mar a thàinig mi a-steach fadalach
is mar a bh' agam ri suidhe aig a' chùl
is nighean an dorais rim thaobh,
's i a' cùnntadh an airgid-inntrigidh ...

Ach tha mi taingeil gun deach mi ann
air sgàth na chuala mi air mo shlighe
air rèidio a' chàir: cuideigin ag ràdh
nach e an toileachas dìth a' chràidh
ach a' mhisneachd a bhith gabhail ris a' chràdh
is a' mhisneachd a bhith a' cumail a' dol ...

'S mar a dh'fhàg mi dubhar nan coilltean air mo chùlaibh,
is mi tèarnadh dhan bhaile dheàrrsach eagarra ud
air rathaidean gu h-obann leathann, soilleir,
bha e mar gu robh mi a' dràibheadh meatafor,
mar gu robh mi fhìn a' gabhail pàirt
ann an taisbeanadh de chiùineas.

At St Andrews Poetry Festival

I was pleased to get to hear the poet,
yet somehow I didn't
what with arriving late
and having to sit at the back
where the girl at the door
was counting the takings ...

But I'm glad I went
for the radio talk I heard on my way
in the car: someone saying that
happiness is not the absence of pain
but the courage to accept pain,
and the courage to move on ...

And as I left dark woods behind me
and swept down to that shining town
on roads suddenly straight and broad,
I seemed to be driving a metaphor,
myself caught up
in some revelation of calm.

The Well

Wi a stevin lyk a stane doon a well
                              yi caa me,
drappin, silent-like, whusslin a wee
tae yirsel an thi sma wund yi mak,
scarce a doistir's fethir, but no yet

plunkit, this plash expandin lyk
a futbaa
oot tae thi rim of thi ring an then
explodin lyk a saft-shankit
rockit, loupin up and oot o thi well
                              tae grab thi
waitin lug o a laddie wha, mebbe
twenty year ago noo, furst leanit
owre an, thru thi criss-cross black gloss
paintit plaits o thi covir, drappit doon

a well in St Andrews Cathedral,
green noo, green across aa thi nave,
a stane,
            a stane drappin an no yet
plunkit is thi stevin Eh hear, whiles,

whan Eh sit back an ken ma daith.

A. B. JACKSON

from *Apocrypha*

The Apocalypse of Judas,
chapter thirteen, verse
something-or-other:

as cows feed on clover,
crows on earthworms,
so men desire digestive charms.

It is beauty sustains us ...
lean cuts from the Cross,
Italian shoes.

Therefore avoid St Andrews,
its burnt crust of a castle,
golf ball truffles,

the West Sands
a mouth-watering prospect for the damned.

MARGARET OLIPHANT

The Library Window

A Story of the Seen and the Unseen

I

I was not aware at first of the many discussions which had gone on about
that window. It was almost opposite one of the windows of the large
old-fashioned drawing-room of the house in which I spent that
summer, which was of so much importance in my life. Our house and
the library were on opposite sides of the broad High Street of St Rule's,
which is a fine street, wide and ample, and very quiet, as strangers think
who come from noisier places; but in a summer evening there is much
coming and going, and the stillness is full of sound – the sound of footsteps and pleasant voices, softened by the summer air. There are even
exceptional moments when it is noisy: the time of the fair, and on
Saturday nights sometimes, and when there are excursion trains. Then
even the softest sunny air of the evening will not smooth the harsh tones
and the stumbling steps; but at these unlovely moments we shut the
windows, and even I, who am so fond of that deep recess where I
can take refuge from all that is going on inside, and make myself
a spectator of all the varied story out of doors, withdraw from my
watch-tower. To tell the truth, there never was very much going on
inside. The house belonged to my aunt, to whom (she says, Thank God!)
nothing ever happens. I believe that many things have happened to her
in her time; but that was all over at the period of which I am speaking,
and she was old, and very quiet. Her life went on in a routine never broken. She got up at the same hour every day, and did the same things
in the same rotation, day by day the same. She said that this was the
greatest support in the world, and that routine is a kind of salvation. It
may be so; but it is a very dull salvation, and I used to feel that I would
rather have incident, whatever kind of incident it might be. But then at
that time I was not old, which makes all the difference.

At the time of which I speak the deep recess of the drawing-room
window was a great comfort to me. Though she was an old lady (perhaps

because she was so old) she was very tolerant, and had a kind of feeling for me. She never said a word, but often gave me a smile when she saw how I had built myself up, with my books and my basket of work. I did very little work, I fear – now and then a few stitches when the spirit moved me, or when I had got well afloat in a dream, and was more tempted to follow it out than to read my book, as sometimes happened. At other times, and if the book were interesting, I used to get through volume after volume sitting there, paying no attention to anybody. And yet I did pay a kind of attention. Aunt Mary's old ladies came in to call, and I heard them talk, though I very seldom listened; but for all that, if they had anything to say that was interesting, it is curious how I found it in my mind afterwards, as if the air had blown it to me. They came and went, and I had the sensation of their old bonnets gliding out and in, and their dresses rustling; and now and then had to jump up and shake hands with some one who knew me, and asked after my papa and mamma. Then Aunt Mary would give me a little smile again, and I slipped back to my window. She never seemed to mind. My mother would not have let me do it, I know. She would have remembered dozens of things there were to do. She would have sent me up-stairs to fetch something which I was quite sure she did not want, or down-stairs to carry some quite unnecessary message to the housemaid. She liked to keep me running about. Perhaps that was one reason why I was so fond of Aunt Mary's drawing-room, and the deep recess of the window, and the curtain that fell half over it, and the broad window-seat, where one could collect so many things without being found fault with for untidiness. Whenever we had anything the matter with us in these days, we were sent to St Rule's to get up our strength. And this was my case at the time of which I am going to speak.

Everybody had said, since ever I learned to speak, that I was fantastic and fanciful and dreamy, and all the other words with which a girl who may happen to like poetry, and to be fond of thinking, is so often made uncomfortable. People don't know what they mean when they say fantastic. It sounds like Madge Wildfire or something of that sort. My mother thought I should always be busy, to keep nonsense out of my head. But really I was not at all fond of nonsense. I was rather serious than otherwise. I would have been no trouble to anybody if I had been left to myself. It was only that I had a sort of second-sight, and was conscious of things to which I paid no attention. Even when reading the most interesting book, the things that were being talked about blew in to me; and I heard what the people were saying in the streets as they passed under the window. Aunt Mary always said I could do two or indeed three things at once – both read and listen, and see. I am sure that I did not listen much, and seldom looked out, of set purpose – as some people do who notice what bonnets the ladies in the street have on; but I did hear what I couldn't help hearing, even when I was reading my book, and I did see all sorts of things, though often for a whole half-hour I might never lift my eyes.

This does not explain what I said at the beginning, that there were many discussions about that window. It was, and still is, the last window in the row, of the College Library, which is opposite my aunt's house in the High Street. Yet it is not exactly opposite, but a little to the west, so that I could see it best from the left side of my recess. I took it calmly for granted that it was a window like any other till I first heard the talk about it which was going on in the drawing-room. 'Have you never made up your mind, Mrs Balcarres,' said old Mr Pitmilly, 'whether that window opposite is a window or no?' He said Mistress Balcarres – and he was always called Mr Pitmilly, Morton: which was the name of his place.

'I am never sure of it, to tell the truth,' said Aunt Mary, 'all these years.'

'Bless me!' said one of the old ladies, 'and what window may that be?'

Mr Pitmilly had a way of laughing as he spoke, which did not please me; but it was true that he was not perhaps desirous of pleasing me. He said, 'Oh, just the window opposite,' with his laugh running through his words; 'our friend can never make up her mind about it, though she has been living opposite it since –'

'You need never mind the date,' said another; 'the Leebrary window! Dear me, what should it be but a window? Up at that height it could not be a door.'

'The question is,' said my aunt, 'if it is a real window with glass in it, or if it is merely painted, or if it once was a window, and has been built up. And the oftener people look at it, the less they are able to say.'

'Let me see this window,' said old Lady Carnbee, who was very active and strong-minded; and then they all came crowding upon me – three or four old ladies, very eager, and Mr Pitmilly's white hair appearing over their heads, and my aunt sitting quiet and smiling behind.

'I mind the window very well,' said Lady Carnbee; 'ay: and so do more than me. But in its present appearance it is just like any other window; but has not been cleaned, I should say, in the memory of man.'

'I see what ye mean,' said one of the others. 'It is just a very dead thing without any reflection in it; but I've seen as bad before.'

'Ay, it's dead enough,' said another, 'but that's no rule; for these hizzies of women-servants in this ill age –'

'Nay, the women are well enough,' said the softest voice of all, which was Aunt Mary's. 'I will never let them risk their lives cleaning the outside of mine. And there are no women-servants in the Old Library: there is maybe something more in it than that.'

They were all pressing into my recess, pressing upon me, a row of old faces, peering into something they could not understand. I had a sense in my mind how curious it was, the wall of old ladies in their old satin gowns all glazed with age, Lady Carnbee with her lace about her head. Nobody was looking at me or thinking of me; but I felt unconsciously the contrast of my youngness to their oldness, and stared at them as they stared over my head at the Library window. I had given it no attention up to this time. I was more taken up with the old ladies than with the thing they were looking at.

'The framework is all right at least, I can see that, and pented black –'

'And the panes are pented black too. It's no window, Mrs Balcarres. It has been filled in, in the days of the window duties: you will mind, Leddy Carnbee.'

'Mind!' said that oldest lady. 'I mind when your mother was marriet, Jeanie: and that's neither the day nor yesterday. But as for the window, it's just a delusion: and that is my opinion of the matter, if you ask me.'

'There's a great want of light in that muckle room at the college,' said another. 'If it was a window, the Leebrary would have more light.'

'One thing is clear,' said one of the younger ones, 'it cannot be a window to see through. It may be filled in or it may be built up, but it is not a window to give light.'

'And who ever heard of a window that was no to see through?' Lady Carnbee said. I was fascinated by the look on her face, which was a curious scornful look as of one who knew more than she chose to say: and then my wandering fancy was caught by her hand as she held it up, throwing back the lace that dropped over it. Lady Carnbee's lace was the chief thing about her – heavy black Spanish lace with large flowers. Everything she wore was trimmed with it. A large veil of it hung over her old bonnet. But her hand coming out of this heavy lace was a curious thing to see. She had very long fingers, very taper, which had been much admired in her youth; and her hand was very white, or rather more than white, pale, bleached, and bloodless, with large blue veins standing up upon the back; and she wore some fine rings, among others a big diamond in an ugly old claw setting. They were too big for her, and were wound round and round with yellow silk to make them keep on: and this little cushion of silk, turned brown with long wearing, had twisted round so that it was more conspicuous than the jewels; while the big diamond blazed underneath in the hollow of her hand, like some dangerous thing hiding and sending out darts of light. The hand, which seemed to come almost to a point, with this strange ornament underneath, clutched at my half-terrified imagination. It too seemed to mean far more than was said. I felt as if it might clutch me with sharp claws, and the lurking, dazzling creature bite – with a sting that would go to the heart.

Presently, however, the circle of the old faces broke up, the old ladies returned to their seats, and Mr Pitmilly, small but very erect, stood up in the midst of them, talking with mild authority like a little oracle among the ladies. Only Lady Carnbee always contradicted the neat, little, old gentleman. She gesticulated, when she talked, like a Frenchwoman, and darted forth that hand of hers with the lace hanging over it, so that I always caught a glimpse of the lurking diamond. I thought she looked like a witch among the comfortable little group which gave such attention to everything Mr Pitmilly said.

'For my part, it is my opinion that there is no window there at all,' he said. 'It's very like the thing that's called in scientific language an optical illusion. It arises generally, if I may use such a word in the presence of ladies, from a liver that is not just in the perfitt order and balance that organ demands – and then you will see things – a blue dog, I remember, was the thing in one case, and in another –'

'The man has gane gyte,' said Lady Carnbee; 'I mind the windows in the Auld Leebrary as long as I mind anything. Is the Leebrary itself an optical illusion too?'

'Na, na,' and 'No, no,' said the old ladies 'a blue dogue would a strange vagary: but the Library we have all kent from our youth,' said one. 'And I mind when the Assemblies were held there one year when the Town Hall was building,' another said.

'It is just a great divert to me,' said Aunt Mary: but what was strange was that she paused there, and said in a low tone, 'now': and then went on again, 'for whoever comes to my house, there are aye discussions about that window. I have never just made up my mind about it myself. Sometimes I think it's a case of these wicked window duties, as you said, Miss Jeanie, when half the windows in our houses were blocked up to save the tax. And then, I think, it may be due to that blank kind of building like the great new buildings on the Earthen Mound in

Edinburgh, where the windows are just ornaments. And then whiles I am sure I can see the glass shining when the sun catches it in the afternoon.'

'You could so easily satisfy yourself, Mrs Balcarres, if you were to –'

'Give a laddie a penny to cast a stone, and see what happens,' said Lady Carnbee.

'But I am not sure that I have any desire to satisfy myself,' Aunt Mary said. And then there was a stir in the room, and I had to come out from my recess and open the door for the old ladies and see them down-stairs, as they all went away following one another. Mr Pitmilly gave his arm to Lady Carnbee, though she was always contradicting him; and so the tea-party dispersed. Aunt Mary came to the head of the stairs with her guests in an old-fashioned gracious way, while I went down with them to see that the maid was ready at the door. When I came back Aunt Mary was still standing in the recess looking out. Returning to my seat she said, with a kind of wistful look, 'Well, honey: and what is your opinion?'

'I have no opinion. I was reading my book all the time,' I said.

'And so you were, honey, and no' very civil; but all the same I ken well you heard every word we said.'

II

It was a night in June; dinner was long over, and had it been winter the maids would have been shutting up the house, and my Aunt Mary preparing to go upstairs to her room. But it was still clear daylight, that daylight out of which the sun has been long gone, and which has no longer any rose reflections, but all has sunk into a pearly neutral tint – a light which is daylight yet is not day. We had taken a turn in the garden after dinner, and now we had returned to what we called our usual occupations. My aunt was reading. The English post had come in, and she had got her 'Times', which was her great diversion. The 'Scotsman' was her morning reading, but she liked her 'Times' at night.

As for me, I too was at my usual occupation, which at that time was doing nothing. I had a book as usual, and was absorbed in it: but I was conscious of all that was going on all the same. The people strolled along the broad pavement, making remarks as they passed under the open window which came up into my story or my dream, and sometimes made me laugh. The tone and the faint sing-song, or rather chant, of the accent, which was 'a wee Fifish,' was novel to me, and associated with holiday, and pleasant; and sometimes they said to each other something that was amusing, and often something that suggested a whole story; but presently they began to drop off, the footsteps slackened, the voices died away. It was getting late, though the clear soft daylight went on and on. All through the lingering evening, which seemed to consist of interminable hours, long but not weary, drawn out as if the spell of the light and the outdoor life might never end, I had now and then, quite unawares, cast a glance at the mysterious window which my aunt and her friends had discussed, as I felt, though I dared not say it even to myself, rather foolishly. It caught my eye without any intention on my part, as I paused, as it were, to take breath, in the flowing and current of undistinguishable thoughts and things from without and within which carried me along. First it occurred to me, with a little sensation of discovery, how absurd to say it was not a window, a living window, one to see through! Why, then, had they never *seen* it, these old folk? I saw as I looked up suddenly the faint greyness as of visible space within – a room behind, certainly – dim, as it was natural a room should be on the other side of the street – quite indefinite: yet so clear that if some one were to come to the window there would be nothing surprising in it. For certainly there was a feeling of space behind the panes which these old half-blind ladies had disputed about whether they were glass or only fictitious panes marked on the wall. How silly! When eyes that could see could make it out in a minute. It was only a greyness at present, but it was unmistakable, a space that went back into gloom, as every room does when you look into it across a street. There were no curtains to show whether it was inhabited or not; but a room – oh, as distinctly as ever room was! I was pleased with myself, but said nothing, while Aunt Mary rustled her paper, waiting for a favourable moment to announce a discovery which settled her problem at once. Then I was carried away upon the stream again, and forgot the window, till somebody threw unawares a word from the outer world, 'I'm goin' hame; it'll soon be dark.' Dark! What was the fool thinking of? It never would be dark if one waited out, wandering in the soft air for hours longer; and then my eyes, acquiring easily that new habit, looked across the way again.

Ah, now! Nobody indeed had come to the window; and no light had been lighted, seeing it was still beautiful to read by – a still, clear, colourless light; but the room inside had certainly widened. I could see the grey space and air a little deeper, and a sort of vision, very dim, of a wall, and something against it; something dark, with the blackness that a solid article, however indistinctly seen, takes in the lighter darkness that is only space – a large, black, dark thing coming out into the grey. I looked more intently, and made sure it was a piece of furniture, either a writing-table or perhaps a large book-case. No doubt it must be the last, since this was part of the old library. I never visited the old College Library, but I had seen such places before, and I could well imagine it to myself. How curious that for all the time these old people had looked at it, they had never seen this before!

It was more silent now, and my eyes, I suppose, had grown dim with gazing, doing my best to make it out, when suddenly Aunt Mary said, 'Will you ring the bell, my dear? I must have my lamp.'

'Your lamp?' I cried, 'when it is still daylight.' But then I gave another look at my window, and perceived with a start that the light had indeed changed: for now I saw nothing. It was still light, but there was so much change in the light that my room, with the grey space and the large shadowy book-case, had gone out, and I saw them no more: for even a Scotch night in June, though it looks as if it would never end, does darken at the last. I had almost cried out, but checked myself, and rang the bell for Aunt Mary, and made up my mind I would say nothing till next morning, when to be sure naturally it would be more clear.

Next morning I rather think I forgot all about it – or was busy: or was more idle than usual: the two things meant nearly the same. At all events I thought no more of the window, though I still sat in my own, opposite to it, but occupied with some other fancy. Aunt Mary's visitors came as usual in the afternoon; but their talk was of other things, and for a day or two nothing at all happened to bring back my thoughts into this channel. It might be nearly a week before the subject came back, and once more it was old Lady Carnbee who set me thinking; not that she said anything upon that particular theme. But she was the last of my aunt's afternoon guests to go away, and when she rose to leave she threw up her hands, with those lively gesticulations which so many old Scotch ladies have. 'My faith!' said she, 'there is that bairn there still like a dream. Is the creature bewitched, Mary Balcarres? and is she bound to sit there by night and by day for the rest of her days? You should mind that there's things about, uncanny for women of our blood.'

I was too much startled at first to recognise that it was of me she was speaking. She was like a figure in a picture, with her pale face the colour of ashes, and the big pattern of the Spanish lace hanging half over it, and her hand held up, with the big diamond blazing at me from the inside of her uplifted palm. It was held up in surprise, but it looked as if it were raised in malediction; and the diamond threw out darts of light and glared and twinkled at me. If it had been in its right place it would not have mattered; but there, in the open of the hand! I started up, half in terror, half in wrath. And then the old lady laughed, and her hand dropped. 'I've wakened you to life, and broke the spell,' she said, nodding her old head at me, while the large black silk flowers of the lace waved and threatened. And she took my arm to go down-stairs, laughing and bidding me be steady, and no' tremble and shake like a broken reed. 'You should be as steady as a rock at your age. I was like a young tree,' she said, leaning so heavily that my willowy girlish frame quivered – 'I was a support to virtue, like Pamela, in my time.'

'Aunt Mary, Lady Carnbee is a witch!' I cried, when I came back.

'Is that what you think, honey? Well: maybe she once was,' said Aunt Mary, whom nothing surprised.

And it was that night once more after dinner, and after the post came in, and the 'Times', that I suddenly saw the library window again. I had seen it every day – and noticed nothing; but to-night, still in a little tumult of mind over Lady Carnbee and her wicked diamond which wished me harm, and her lace which waved threats and warnings at me, I looked across the street, and there I saw quite plainly the room opposite, far more clear than before. I saw dimly that it must be a large room, and that the big piece of furniture against the wall was a writing-desk. That in a moment, when first my eyes rested upon it, was quite clear: a large old-fashioned escritoire, standing out into the room: and I knew by the shape of it that it had a great many pigeon-holes and little drawers in the back, and a large table for writing. There was one just like it in my father's library at home. It was such a surprise to see it all so clearly that I closed my eyes, for the moment almost giddy, wondering how papa's desk could have come here – and then when I reminded myself that this was nonsense, and that there were many such writing-tables besides papa's, and looked again – lo! it had all become quite vague and indistinct as it was at first; and I saw nothing but the blank window, of which the old ladies could never be certain whether it was filled up to avoid the window-tax, or whether it had ever been a window at all.

This occupied my mind very much, and yet I did not say anything to Aunt Mary. For one thing, I rarely saw anything at all in the early part of the day; but then that is natural: you can never see into a place from outside, whether it is an empty room or a looking-glass, or people's eyes, or anything else that is mysterious, in the day. It has, I suppose, something to do with the light. But in the evening in June in Scotland – then is the time to see. For it is daylight, yet it is not day, and there is a quality in it which I cannot describe, it is so clear, as if every object was a reflection of itself.

I used to see more and more of the room as the days went on. The large escritoire stood out more and more into the space: with sometimes white glimmering things, which looked like papers, lying on it: and once or twice I was sure I saw a pile of books on the floor close to the writing-table, as if they had gilding upon them in broken specks, like old books. It was always about the time when the lads in the street began to call to each other that they were going home, and sometimes a shriller voice would come from one of the doors, bidding somebody to 'cry upon the laddies' to come back to their suppers. That was always the time I saw best, though it was close upon the moment when the veil seemed to fall and the clear radiance became less living, and all the sounds died out of the street, and Aunt Mary said in her soft voice, 'Honey! Will you ring for the lamp?' She said honey as people say darling: and I think it is a prettier word.

Then finally, while I sat one evening with my book in my hand, looking straight across the street, not distracted by anything, I saw a little movement within. It was not any one visible – but everybody must know what it is to see the stir in the air, the little disturbance – you cannot tell what it is, but that it indicates some one there, even though you can see no one. Perhaps it is a shadow making just one flicker in the still place. You may look at an empty room and the furniture in it for hours, and then suddenly there will be the flicker, and you know that something has come into it. It might only be a dog or a cat; it might be, if that were possible, a bird flying across; but it is some one, something living, which is so different, so completely different, in a moment from the things that are not living. It seemed to strike quite through me, and I gave a little cry. Then Aunt Mary stirred a little, and put down the huge newspaper that almost covered her from sight, and said, 'What is it, honey?' I cried, 'Nothing,' with a little gasp, quickly, for I did not want to be disturbed just at this moment when somebody was coming!

But I suppose she was not satisfied, for she got up and stood behind to see what it was, putting her hand on my shoulder. It was the softest touch in the world, but I could have flung it off angrily: for that moment everything was still again, and the place grew grey and I saw no more.

'Nothing,' I repeated, but I was so vexed I could have cried. 'I told you it was nothing, Aunt Mary. Don't you believe me, that you come to look – and spoil it all!'

I did not mean of course to say these last words; they were forced out of me. I was so much annoyed to see it all melt away like a dream: for it was no dream, but as real as – as real as – myself or anything I ever saw.

She gave my shoulder a little pat with her hand. 'Honey,' she said, 'were you looking at something? Is't that? Is't that?' 'Is it what?' I wanted to say, shaking off her hand, but something in me stopped me: for I said nothing at all, and she went quietly back to her place. I suppose she must have rung the bell herself, for immediately I felt the soft flood of the light behind me, and the evening outside dimmed down, as it did every night, and I saw nothing more.

It was next day, I think, in the afternoon that I spoke. It was brought on by something she said about her fine work. 'I get a mist before my eyes,' she said; 'you will have to learn my old lace stitches, honey – for I soon will not see to draw the threads.'

'Oh I hope you will keep your sight,' I cried, without thinking what I was saying. I was then young and very matter-of-fact. I had not found out that one may mean something, yet not half or a hundredth part of what one seems to mean: and even then probably hoping to be contradicted if it is anyhow against one's self.

'My sight!' she said, looking up at me with a look that was almost angry; 'there is no question of losing my sight – on the contrary, my eyes are very strong. I may not see to draw fine threads, but I see at a distance as well as ever I did – as well as you do.'

'I did not mean any harm, Aunt Mary,' I said. 'I thought you said – But how can your sight be as good as ever when you are in doubt about that window? I can see into the room as clear as –' My voice wavered, for I had just looked up and across the street, and I could have sworn that there was no window at all, but only a false image of one painted on the wall.

'Ah!' she said, with a little tone of keenness and of surprise: and she half rose up, throwing down her work hastily, as if she meant to come to me: then, perhaps seeing the bewildered look on my face, she paused and hesitated – 'Ay, honey!' she said, 'Have you got so far ben as that?'

What did she mean? Of course I knew all the old Scotch phrases as well as I knew myself; but it is a comfort to take refuge in a little ignorance, and I know I pretended not to understand whenever I was put out. 'I don't know what you mean by "far ben".' I cried out, very impatient. I don't know what might have followed, but some one just then came to call, and she could only give me a look before she went forward, putting out her hand to her visitor. It was a very soft look, but anxious, and as if she did not know what to do: and she shook her head a very little, and I thought, though there was a smile on her face, there was something wet about her eyes. I retired into my recess, and nothing more was said.

But it was very tantalising that it should fluctuate so; for sometimes I saw that room quite plain and clear – quite as clear as I could see papa's library, for example, when I shut my eyes. I compared it naturally to my father's study, because of the shape of the writing-table, which, as I tell you, was the same as his. At times I saw the papers on the table quite plain, just as I had seen his papers many a day. And the little pile of books on the floor at the foot – not ranged regularly in order, but put down one above the other, with all their angles going different ways, and a speck of the old gilding shining here and there. And then again at other times I saw nothing, absolutely nothing, and was no better than the old ladies who had peered over my head, drawing their eyelids together, and arguing that the window had been shut up because of the old long-abolished window tax, or else that it had never been a window at all. It annoyed me very much at those dull moments to feel that I too puckered up my eyelids and saw no better than they.

Aunt Mary's old ladies came and went day after day while June went on. I was to go back in July, and I felt that I should be very unwilling indeed to leave until I had quite cleared up – as I was indeed in the way of doing – the mystery of that window which changed so strangely and appeared quite a different thing, not only to different people, but to the same eyes at different times. Of course I said to myself it must simply be an effect of the light. And yet I did not quite like that explanation either, but would have been better pleased to make out to myself that it was some superiority in me which made it so clear to me, if it were only the great superiority of young eyes over old – though that was not quite enough to satisfy me, seeing it was a superiority which I shared with every little lass and lad in the street. I rather wanted, I believe, to think that there was some particular insight in me which gave clearness to my sight – which was a most impertinent assumption, but really did not mean half the harm it seems to mean when it is put down here in black and white. I had several times again, however, seen the room quite plain, and made out that it was a large room, with a great picture in a dim gilded frame hanging on the farther wall, and many other pieces of solid furniture making a blackness here and there, besides the great escritoire against the wall, which had evidently been placed near the window for the sake of the light. One thing became visible to me after another, till I almost thought I should end by being able to read the old lettering on one of the big volumes which projected from the others and caught the light; but this was all preliminary to the great event which happened about Midsummer Day – the day of St John, which was once so much thought of as a festival, but now means nothing at all in Scotland any more than any other of the saints' days: which I shall always think a great pity and loss to Scotland, whatever Aunt Mary may say.

III

It was about midsummer, I cannot say exactly to a day when, but near that time, when the great event happened. I had grown very well acquainted by this time with that large dim room. Not only the escritoire, which was very plain to me now, with the papers upon it, and the books at its foot, but the great picture that hung against the farther wall, and various other shadowy pieces of furniture, especially a chair which one evening I saw had been moved into the space before the escritoire, – a little change which made my heart beat, for it spoke so distinctly of some one who must have been there, the some one who had already made me start, two or three times before, by some vague shadow of him or thrill of him which made a sort of movement in the silent space: a movement which made me sure that next minute I must see something or hear something which would explain the whole – if it were not that something always happened outside to stop it, at the very moment of its accomplishment. I had no warning this time of movement or shadow. I had been looking into the room very attentively a little while before, and had made out everything almost clearer than ever; and then had bent my attention again on my book, and read a chapter or two at a most exciting period of the story: and consequently had quite left St Rule's, and the High Street, and the College Library, and was really in a South American forest, almost throttled by the flowery creepers, and treading softly lest I should put my foot on a scorpion or a dangerous snake. At this moment, something suddenly calling my attention to the outside, I looked across, and then, with a start, sprang up, for I could not contain myself. I don't know what I said, but enough to startle the people in the room, one of whom was old Mr Pitmilly. They all looked round upon me to ask what was the matter. And when I gave my usual answer of 'Nothing', sitting down again shamefaced but very much excited, Mr Pitmilly got up and came forward, and looked out, apparently to see what was the cause. He saw nothing, for he went back again, and I could hear him telling Aunt Mary not to be alarmed, for Missy had fallen into a doze with the heat, and had startled herself waking up, at which they all laughed: another time I could have killed him for his impertinence, but my mind was too much taken up now to pay any attention. My head was throbbing and my heart beating. I was in such high excitement, however, that to restrain myself completely, to be perfectly silent, was more easy to me then than at any other time of my life. I waited until the old gentleman had taken his seat again, and then I looked back. Yes, there he was! I had not been deceived. I knew then, when I looked across, that this was what I had been looking for all the time – that I had known he was there, and had been waiting for him, every time there was that flicker of movement in the room – him and no one else. And there at last, just as I had expected, he was. I don't know that in reality I ever had expected him, or any one: but this was what I felt when, suddenly looking into that curious dim room, I saw him there.

He was sitting in the chair, which he must have placed for himself, or which some one else in the dead of night when nobody was looking must have set for him, in front of the escritoire – with the back of his head towards me, writing. The light fell upon him from the left hand, and therefore upon his shoulders and the side of his head, which, however, was too much turned away to show anything of his face. Oh, how strange that there should be some one staring at him as I was doing, and he never to turn his head, to make a movement! If any one stood and looked at me, were I in the soundest sleep that ever was, I would wake, I would jump up, I would feel it through everything. But there he sat and never moved. You are not to suppose, though I said the light fell upon him from the left hand, that there was very much light. There never is in a room you are looking into like that across the street; but there was enough to see him by – the outline of his figure dark and solid, seated in the chair, and the fairness of his head visible faintly, a clear spot against the dimness. I saw this outline against the dim gilding of the frame of the large picture which hung on the farther wall.

I sat all the time the visitors were there, in a sort of rapture, gazing at this figure. I knew no reason why I should be so much moved. In an ordinary way, to see a student at an opposite window quietly doing his work might have interested me a little, but certainly it would not have moved me in any such way. It is always interesting to have a glimpse like this of an unknown life – to see so much and yet know so little, and to wonder, perhaps, what the man is doing, and why he never turns his head. One would go to the window – but not too close, lest he should see you and think you were spying upon him – and one would ask, is he still there? is he writing, writing always? I wonder what he is writing! And it would be a great amusement: but no more. This was not my feeling at all in the present case. It was a sort of breathless watch, an absorption. I did not feel that I had eyes for anything else, or any room in my mind for another thought. I no longer heard, as I generally did, the stories and the wise remarks (or foolish) of Aunt Mary's old ladies or Mr Pitmilly. I heard only a murmur behind me, the interchange of voices, one softer, one sharper; but it was not as in the time when I sat reading and heard every word, till the story in my book, and the stories they were telling (what they said almost always shaped into stories), were all mingled into each other, and the hero in the novel became somehow the hero (or more likely heroine) of them all. But I took no notice of what they were saying now. And it was not that there was anything very interesting to look at, except the fact that he was there. He did nothing to keep up the absorption of my thoughts. He moved just so much as a man will do when he is very busily writing, thinking of nothing else. There was a faint turn of his head as he went from one side to another of the page he was writing; but it appeared to be a long long page which never wanted turning. Just a little inclination when he was at the end of the line, outward, and then a little inclination inward when he began the next. That was little enough to keep one gazing. But I suppose it was the gradual course of events leading up to this, the finding out of one thing after another as the eyes got accustomed to the vague light: first the room itself, and then the writing-table, and then the other furniture, and last of all the human inhabitant who gave it all meaning. This was all so interesting that it was like a country which one had discovered. And then the extraordinary blindness of the other people who disputed among themselves whether it was a window at all! I did not, I am sure, wish to be disrespectful, and I was very fond of my Aunt Mary, and I liked Mr Pitmilly well enough, and I was afraid of Lady Carnbee. But yet to think of the – I know I ought not to say stupidity – the blindness of them, the foolishness, the insensibility! discussing it as if a thing that your eyes could see was a thing to discuss! It would have been unkind to think it was because they were old and their faculties dimmed. It is so sad to think that the faculties grow dim, that such a woman as my Aunt Mary should fail in seeing, or hearing, or feeling, that I would not have dwelt on it for a moment, it would have seemed so cruel! And then such a clever old lady as Lady Carnbee, who could see through a millstone, people said – and Mr Pitmilly, such an old man of the world. It did indeed bring tears to my eyes to think that all those clever people, solely by reason of being no longer young as I was, should have the simplest things shut out from them; and for all their wisdom and their knowledge be unable to see what a girl like me could see so easily. I was too much grieved for them to dwell upon that thought, and half ashamed, though perhaps half proud too, to be so much better off than they.

All those thoughts flitted through my mind as I sat and gazed across the street. And I felt there was so much going in that room across the street! He was so absorbed in his writing, never looked up, never paused for a word, never turned round in his chair, or got up and walked about the room as my father did. Papa is a great writer, everybody says: but he would have come to the window and looked out, he would have drummed with his fingers on the pane, he would have watched a fly and helped it over a difficulty, and played with the fringe of the curtain, and done a dozen other nice, pleasant, foolish things, till the next sentence took shape. 'My dear, I am waiting for a word,' he would say to my mother when she looked at him, with a question why he was so idle, in her eyes; and then he would laugh, and go back again to his writing-table. But He over there never stopped at all. It was like a fascination. I could not take my eyes from him and that little scarcely perceptible movement he made, turning his head. I trembled with impatience to see him turn the page, or perhaps throw down his finished sheet on the floor, as somebody looking into a window like me once saw Sir Walter do, sheet after sheet. I should have cried out if this Unknown had done that. I should not have been able to help myself, whoever had been present; and gradually I got into such a state of suspense waiting for it to be done that my head grew hot and my hands cold. And then, just when there was a little movement of his elbow, as if he were about to do this, to be called away by Aunt Mary to see Lady Carnbee to the door! I believe I did not hear her till she had called me three times, and then I stumbled up, all flushed and hot, and nearly crying. When I came out from the recess to give the old lady my arm (Mr Pitmilly had gone away some time before), she put up her hand and stroked my cheek. 'What ails the bairn?' she said; 'she's fevered. You must not let her sit her lane in the window, Mary Balcarres. You and me know what comes of that.' Her old fingers had a strange touch, cold like something not living, and I felt that dreadful diamond sting me on the cheek.

I do not say that this was not just a part of my excitement and suspense; and I know it is enough to make any one laugh when the excitement was all about an unknown man writing in a room on the other side of the way, and my impatience because he never came to an end of the page. If you think I was not quite as well aware of this as any one could be! But the worst was that this dreadful old lady felt my heart beating against her arm that was within mine. 'You are just in a dream,' she said to me, with her old voice close at my ear as we went down-stairs. 'I don't know who it is about, but it's bound to be some man that is not worth it. If you were wise you would think of him no more.'

'I am thinking of no man!' I said, half crying. 'It is very unkind and dreadful of you to say so, Lady Carnbee. I never thought of – any man, in all my life!' I cried in a passion of indignation. The old lady clung tighter to my arm, and pressed it to her, not unkindly.

'Poor little bird,' she said, 'how it's strugglin' and flutterin'! I'm not saying but what it's more dangerous when it's all for a dream.'

She was not at all unkind; but I was very angry and excited, and would scarcely shake that old pale hand which she put out to me from her carriage window when I had helped her in. I was angry with her, and I was afraid of the diamond, which looked up from under her finger as if it saw through and through me; and whether you believe me or not, I am certain that it stung me again – a sharp malignant prick, oh full of meaning! She never wore gloves, but only black lace mittens, through which that horrible diamond gleamed.

I ran up-stairs – she had been the last to go – and Aunt Mary too had gone to get ready for dinner, for it was late. I hurried to my place, and looked across, with my heart beating more than ever. I made quite sure I should see the finished sheet lying white upon the floor. But what I gazed at was only the dim blank of that window which they said was no window. The light had changed in some wonderful way during that five minutes I had been gone, and there was nothing, nothing, not a reflection, not a glimmer. It looked exactly as they all said, the blank form of a window painted on the wall. It was too much: I sat down in my excitement and cried as if my heart would break. I felt that they had done something to it, that it was not natural, that I could not bear their unkindness – even Aunt Mary. They thought it not good for me! not good for me! and they had done something – even Aunt Mary herself – and that wicked diamond that hid itself in Lady Carnbee's hand. Of course I knew all this was ridiculous as well as you could tell me; but I was exasperated by the disappointment and the sudden stop to all my excited feelings, and I could not bear it. It was more strong than I.

I was late for dinner, and naturally there were some traces in my eyes that I had been crying when I came into the full light in the dining-room, where Aunt Mary could look at me at her pleasure, and I could not run away. She said, 'Honey, you have been shedding tears. I'm loth, loth that a bairn of your mother's should be made to shed tears in my house.'

'I have not been made to shed tears,' cried I; and then, to save myself another fit of crying, I burst out laughing and said, 'I am afraid of that dreadful diamond on old Lady Carnbee's hand. It bites – I am sure it bites! Aunt Mary, look here.'

'You foolish lassie,' Aunt Mary said; but she looked at my cheek under the light of the lamp, and then she gave it a little pat with her soft hand. 'Go away with you, you silly bairn. There is no bite; but a flushed cheek, my honey, and a wet eye. You must just read out my paper to me after dinner when the post is in: and we'll have no more thinking and no more dreaming for tonight.'

'Yes, Aunt Mary,' said I. But I knew what would happen; for when she opens up her 'Times', all full of the news of the world, and the speeches and things which she takes an interest in, though I cannot tell why – she forgets. And as I kept very quiet and made not a sound, she forgot to-night what she had said, and the curtain hung a little more over me than usual, and I sat down in my recess as if I had been a hundred miles away. And my heart gave a great jump, as if it would have come out of my breast; for he was there. But not as he had been in the morning – I suppose the light, perhaps, was not good enough to go on with his work without a lamp or candles – for he had turned away from the table and was fronting the window, sitting leaning back in his chair, and turning his head to me. Not to me – he knew nothing about me. I thought he was not looking at anything; but with his face turned my way. My heart was in my mouth: it was so unexpected, so strange! though why it should have seemed strange I know not, for there was no communication between him and me that it should have moved me; and what could be more natural than that a man, wearied of his work, and feeling the want perhaps of more light, and yet that it was not dark enough to light a lamp, should turn round in his own chair, and rest a little, and think – perhaps of nothing at all? Papa always says he is thinking of nothing at all. He says things blow through his mind as if the doors were open, and he has no responsibility. What sort of things were blowing through this man's mind? or was he thinking, still thinking, of what he had been writing and going on with it still? The thing that troubled me most was that I could not make out his face. It is very difficult to do so when you see a person only through two windows, your own and his. I wanted very much to recognise him afterwards if I should chance to meet him in the street. If he had only stood up and moved about the room, I should have made out the rest of his figure, and then I should have known him again; or if he had only come to the window (as papa always did), then I should have seen his face clearly enough to have recognised him. But, to be sure, he did not see any need to do anything in order that I might recognise him, for he did not know I existed; and probably if he had known I was watching him, he would have been annoyed and gone away.

But he was as immovable there facing the window as he had been seated at the desk. Sometimes he made a little faint stir with a hand or a foot, and I held my breath, hoping he was about to rise from his chair – but he never did it. And with all the efforts I made I could not be sure of his face. I puckered my eyelids together as old Miss Jeanie did who was shortsighted, and I put my hands on each side of my face to concentrate the light on him: but it was all in vain. Either the face changed as I sat staring, or else it was the light that was not good enough, or I don't know what it was. His hair seemed to me light – certainly there was no dark line about his head, as there would have been had it been very dark – and I saw, where it came across the old gilt frame on the wall behind, that it must be fair: and I am almost sure he had no beard. Indeed I am sure that he had no beard, for the outline of his face was distinct enough; and the daylight was still quite clear out of doors, so that I recognised perfectly a baker's boy who was on the pavement opposite, and whom I should have known again whenever I had met him: as if it was of the least importance to recognise a baker's boy! There was one thing, however, rather curious about this boy. He had been throwing stones at something or somebody. In St Rule's they have a great way of throwing stones at each other, and I suppose there had been a battle. I suppose also that he had one stone in his hand left over from the battle, and his roving eye took in all the incidents of the street to judge where he could throw it with most effect and mischief. But apparently he found nothing worthy of it in the street, for he suddenly turned round with a flick under his leg to show his cleverness, and aimed it straight at the window. I remarked without remarking that it struck with a hard sound and without any breaking of glass, and fell straight down on the pavement. But I took no notice of this even in my mind, so intently was I watching the figure within, which moved not nor took the slightest notice, and remained just as dimly clear, as perfectly seen, yet as indistinguishable, as before. And then the light began to fail a little, not diminishing the prospect within but making it still less distinct than it had been.

Then I jumped up, feeling Aunt Mary's hand upon my shoulder. 'Honey,' she said, 'I asked you twice to ring the bell; but you did not hear me.'

'Oh, Aunt Mary!' I cried in great penitence, but turning again to the window in spite of myself.

'You must come away from there: you must come away from there,' she said, almost as if she were angry: and then her soft voice grew softer, and she gave me a kiss: 'never mind about the lamp, honey; I have rung myself, and it is coming; but, silly bairn, you must not aye be dreaming – your little head will turn.'

All the answer I made, for I could scarcely speak, was to give a little wave with my hand to the window on the other side of the street.

She stood there patting me softly on the shoulder for a whole minute or more, murmuring something that sounded like, 'She must go away, she must go away.' Then she said, always with her hand soft on my shoulder, 'Like a dream when one awaketh.' And when I looked again, I saw the blank of an opaque surface and nothing more.

Aunt Mary asked me no more questions. She made me come into the room and sit in the light and read something to her. But I did not know what I was reading, for there suddenly came into my mind and took possession of it, the thud of the stone upon the window, and its descent straight down, as if from some hard substance that threw it off: though I had myself seen it strike upon the glass of the panes across the way.

IV

I am afraid I continued in a state of great exaltation and commotion of mind for some time. I used to hurry through the day till the evening came, when I could watch my neighbour through the window opposite. I did not talk much to any one, and I never said a word about my own questions and wonderings. I wondered who he was, what he was doing, and why he never came till the evening (or very rarely); and I also wondered much to what house the room belonged in which he sat. It seemed to form a portion of the old College Library, as I have often said. The window was one of the line of windows which I understood lighted the large hall; but whether this room belonged to the library itself, or how its occupant gained access to it, I could not tell. I made up my mind that it must open out of the hall, and that the gentleman must be the Librarian or one of his assistants, perhaps kept busy all the day in his official duties, and only able to get to his desk and do his own private work in the evening. One has heard of so many things like that – a man who had to take up some other kind of work for his living, and then when his leisure-time came, gave it all up to something he really loved – some study or some book he was writing. My father himself at one time had been like that. He had been in the Treasury all day, and then in the evening wrote his books, which made him famous. His daughter, however little she might know of other things, could not but know that! But it discouraged me very much when somebody pointed out to me one day in the street an old gentleman who wore a wig and took a great deal of snuff, and said, That's the Librarian of the old College. It gave me a great shock for a moment; but then I remembered that an old gentleman has generally assistants, and that it must be one of them.

Gradually I became quite sure of this. There was another small window above, which twinkled very much when the sun shone, and looked a very kindly bright little window, above that dullness of the other which hid so much. I made up my mind this was the window of his other room, and that these two chambers at the end of the beautiful hall were really beautiful for him to live in, so near all the books, and so retired and quiet, that nobody knew of them. What a fine thing for him! And you could see what use he made of his good fortune as he sat there, so constant at his writing for hours together. Was it a book he was writing, or could it be perhaps Poems? This was a thought which made my heart beat; but I concluded with much regret that it could not be Poems, because no one could possible write Poems like that, straight off, without pausing for a word or a rhyme. Had they been Poems he must have risen up, he must have paced about the room or come to the window as papa did – not that papa wrote Poems: he always said, 'I am not worthy even to speak of such prevailing mysteries,' shaking his head – which gave me a wonderful admiration and almost awe of a Poet, who was thus much greater even than papa. But I could not believe that a poet could have kept still for hours and hours like that. What could it be then? Perhaps it was history; that is a great thing to work at, but you would not perhaps need to move nor to stride up and down, or look out upon the sky and the wonderful light.

He did move now and then, however, though he never came to the window. Sometimes, as I have said, he would turn round in his chair and turn his face towards it, and sit there for a long time musing when the light had begun to fail, and the world was full of that strange day which was night, that light without colour, in which everything was so clearly visible, and there were no shadows. 'It was between the night and the day, when the fairy folk have power.' This was the after-light of the wonderful, long, long summer evening, the light without shadows. It had a spell in it, and sometimes it made me afraid: and all manner of strange thoughts seemed to come in, and I always felt that if only we had a little more vision in our eyes we might see beautiful folk walking about in it, who were not of our world. I thought most likely he saw them, from the way he sat there looking out: and this made my heart expand with the most curious sensation, as if of pride that, though I could not see, he did, and did not even require to come to the window, as I did, sitting close in the depth of the recess, with my eyes upon him, and almost seeing things through his eyes.

I was so much absorbed in these thoughts and in watching him every evening – for now he never missed an evening, but was always there – that people began to remark that I was looking pale and that I could not be well, for I paid no attention when they talked to me, and did not care to go out, nor to join the other girls for their tennis, nor to do anything that others did; and some said to Aunt Mary that I was quickly losing all the ground I had gained, and that she could never send me back to my mother with a white face like that. Aunt Mary had begun to look at me anxiously for some time before that, and, I am sure, held secret consultations over me, sometimes with the doctor, and sometimes with her old ladies, who thought they knew more about young girls than even the doctors. And I could hear them saying to her that I wanted diversion, that I must be diverted, and that she must take me out more, and give a party, and that when the summer visitors began to come there would perhaps be a ball or two, or Lady Carnbee would get up a picnic. 'And there's my young lord coming home,' said the old lady whom they called Miss Jeanie, 'and I never knew the young lassie yet that would not cock up her bonnet at the sight of a young lord.'

But Aunt Mary shook her head. 'I would not lippen much to the young lord,' she said. 'His mother is sore set upon siller for him; and my poor bit honey has no fortune to speak of. No, we must not fly so high as the young lord; but I will gladly take her about the country to see the old castles and towers. It will perhaps rouse her up a little.'

'And if that does not answer we must think of something else,' the old lady said.

I heard them perhaps that day because they were talking of me, which is always so effective a way of making you hear – for latterly I had not been paying any attention to what they were saying; and I thought to myself how little they knew, and how little I cared about even the old castles and curious houses, having something else in my mind. But just about that time Mr Pitmilly came in, who was always a friend to me, and, when he heard them talking, he managed to stop them and turn the conversation into another channel. And after a while, when the ladies were gone away, he came up to my recess, and gave a glance right over my head. And then he asked my Aunt Mary if ever she had settled her question about the window opposite, 'that you thought was a window sometimes, and then not a window, and many curious things,' the old gentleman said.

My Aunt Mary gave me another very wistful look; and then she said, 'Indeed, Mr Pitmilly, we are just where we were, and I am quite as unsettled as ever; and I think my niece she has taken up my views, for I see her many a time looking across and wondering, and I am not clear now what her opinion is.'

'My opinion!' I said, 'Aunt Mary.' I could not help being a little scornful, as one is when one is very young. 'I have no opinion. There is not only a window but there is a room, and I could show you –' I was going to say, 'show you the gentleman who sits and writes in it,' but I stopped, not knowing what they might say, and looked from one to another. 'I could tell you – all the furniture that is in it,' I said. And then I felt something like a flame that went over my face, and that all at once my cheeks were burning. I thought they gave a little glance at each other, but that may have been folly. 'There is a great picture, in a big dim frame,' I said, feeling a little breathless, 'on the wall opposite the window –'

'Is there so?' said Mr Pitmilly, with a little laugh. And he said,

'Now I will tell you what we'll do. You know that there is a conversation party, or whatever they call it, in the big room tonight, and it will be all open and lighted up. And it is a handsome room, and two-three things well worth looking at. I will just step along after we have all got our dinner, and take you over to the pairty, madam – Missy and you –'

'Dear me!' said Aunt Mary. 'I have not gone to a pairty for more years than I would like to say – and never once to the Library Hall.' Then she gave a little shiver, and said quite low, 'I could not go there.'

'Then you will just begin again to-night, madam,' said Mr Pitmilly, taking no notice of this, 'and a proud man will I be leading in Mistress Balcarres that was once the pride of the ball!'

'Ah, once!' said Aunt Mary, with a low little laugh and then a sigh. 'And we'll not say how long ago'; and after that she made a pause, looking always at me: and then she said, 'I accept your offer, and we'll put on our braws; and I hope you will have no occasion to think shame of us. But why not take your dinner here?'

That was how it was settled, and the old gentleman went away to dress, looking quite pleased. But I came to Aunt Mary as soon as he was gone, and besought her not to make me go. 'I like the long bonnie night and the light that lasts so long. And I cannot bear to dress up and go out, wasting it all in a stupid party. I hate parties, Aunt Mary!' I cried, 'and I would far rather stay here.'

'My honey,' she said, taking both my hands, 'I know it will maybe be a blow to you, – but it's better so.'

'How could it be a blow to me?' I cried; 'but I would far rather not go.'

'You'll just go with me, honey, just this once: it is not often I go out. You will go with me this one night, just this one night, my honey sweet.'

I am sure there were tears in Aunt Mary's eyes, and she kissed me between the words. There was nothing more that I could say; but how I grudged the evening! A mere party, a conversazione (when all the College was away, too, and nobody to make conversation!), instead of my enchanted hour at my window and the soft strange light, and the dim face looking out, which kept me wondering and wondering what was he thinking of, what was he looking for, who was he? all one wonder and mystery and question, through the long, long, slowly fading night!

It occurred to me, however, when I was dressing – though I was so sure that he would prefer his solitude to everything – that he might perhaps, it was just possible, be there. And when I thought of that, I took out my white frock – though Janet had laid out my blue one – and my little pearl necklace which I thought was too good to wear. They were not very large pearls, but they were real pearls, and very even and lustrous though they were small; and though I did not think much of my appearance then, there must have been something about me – pale as I was but apt to colour in a moment, with my dress so white, and my pearls so white, and my hair all shadowy – perhaps, that was pleasant to look at: for even old Mr Pitmilly had a strange look in his eyes, as if he was not only pleased but sorry too, perhaps thinking me a creature that would have troubles in this life, though I was so young and knew them not. And when Aunt Mary looked at me, there was a little quiver about her mouth. She herself had on her pretty lace and her white hair very nicely done, and looking her best. As for Mr Pitmilly, he had a beautiful fine French cambric frill to his shirt, plaited in the most minute plaits, and with a diamond pin in it which sparkled as much as Lady Carnbee's ring; but this was a fine frank kindly stone, that looked you straight in the face and sparkled, with the light dancing in it as if it were pleased to see you, and to be shining on that old gentleman's honest and faithful breast: for he had been one of Aunt Mary's lovers in their early days, and still thought there was nobody like her in the world.

I had got into quite a happy commotion of mind by the time we set out across the street in the soft light of the evening to the Library Hall. Perhaps, after all, I should see him, and see the room which I was so well acquainted with, and find out why he sat there so constantly and never was seen abroad. I though I might even hear what he was working at, which would be such a pleasant thing to tell papa when I went home. A friend of mine at St Rule's – oh, far, far more busy than you ever were, papa! – and then my father would laugh as he always did, and say he was but an idler and never busy at all.

The room was all light and bright, flowers wherever flowers could be, and the long lines of the books that went along the walls on each side, lighting up wherever there was a line of gilding or an ornament, with a little response. It dazzled me at first all that light: but I was very eager, though I kept very quiet, looking round to see if perhaps in any corner, in the middle of any group, he would be there. I did not expect to see him among the ladies. He would not be with them, – he was too studious, too silent: but, perhaps among that circle of grey heads at the upper end of the room – perhaps –

No: I am not sure that it was not half a pleasure to me to make quite sure that there was not one whom I could take for him, who was at all like my vague image of him. No: it was absurd to think that he would be here, amid all that sound of voices, under the glare of that light. I felt a little proud to think that he was in his room as usual, doing his work, or thinking so deeply over it, as when he turned round in his chair with his face to the light.

I was thus getting a little composed and quiet in my mind, for now that the expectation of seeing him was over, though it was a disappointment, it was a satisfaction too – when Mr Pitmilly came up to me, holding out his arm. 'Now,' he said, 'I am going to take you to see the curiosities.' I thought to myself that after I had seen them and spoken to everybody I knew, Aunt Mary would let me go home, so I went very willingly, though I did not care for the curiosities. Something, however, struck me strangely as we walked up the room. It was the air, rather fresh and strong, from an open window at the east end of the hall. How should there be a window there? I hardly saw what it meant for the first moment, but it blew in my face as if there was some meaning in it, and I felt very uneasy without seeing why.

Then there was another thing that startled me. On that side of the wall which was to the street there seemed no windows at all. A long line of book-cases filled it from end to end. I could not see what that meant either, but it confused me. I was altogether confused. I felt as if I was in a strange country, not knowing where I was going, not knowing what I might find out next. If there were no windows on the wall to the street, where was my window? My heart, which had been jumping up and calming down again all this time, gave a great leap at this, as if it would have come out of me – but I did not know what it could mean.

Then we stopped before a glass case, and Mr Pitmilly showed me some things in it. I could not pay much attention to them. My head was going round and round. I heard his voice going on, and then myself speaking with a queer sound that was hollow in my ears; but I did not know what I was saying or what he was saying. Then he took me to the very end of the room, the east end, saying something that I caught – that I was pale, that the air would do me good. The air was flowing full on me, lifting the lace of my dress, lifting my hair, almost chilly. The window opened into the pale daylight, into the little lane that ran by the end of the building. Mr Pitmilly went on talking, but I could not make out a word he said. Then I heard my own voice, speaking through it, though I did not seem to be aware that I was speaking. 'Where is my window? – where, then, is my window?' I seemed to be saying, and I turned right round, dragging him with me, still holding his arm. As I did this my eye fell upon something at last which I knew. It was a large picture in a broad frame, hanging against the farther wall.

What did it mean? Oh, what did it mean? I turned round again to the open window at the east end, and to the daylight, the strange light without any shadow, that was all round about this lighted hall, holding it like a bubble that would burst, like something that was not real. The real place was the room I knew, in which that picture was hanging, where the writing-table was, and where he sat with his face to the light. But where was the light and the window through which it came? I think my senses must have left me. I went up to the picture which

I knew, and then I walked straight across the room, always dragging Mr Pitmilly, whose face was pale, but who did not struggle but allowed me to lead him, straight across to the where the window was – where the window was not; – where there was no sign of it. 'Where is my window? – where is my window?' I said. And all the time I was sure that I was in a dream, and these lights were all some theatrical illusion, and the people talking; and nothing real but the pale, pale, watching, lingering day standing by to wait until that foolish bubble should burst.

'My dear,' said Mr Pitmilly, 'my dear! Mind that you are in public. Mind where you are. You must not make an outcry and frighten your Aunt Mary. Come away with me. Come away, my dear young lady! and you'll take a seat for a minute or two and compose yourself; and I'll get you an ice or a little wine.' He kept patting my hand, which was on his arm, and looking at me very anxiously. 'Bless me! bless me! I never thought it would have this effect,' he said.

But I would not allow him to take me away in that direction. I went to the picture again and looked at it without seeing it: and then I went across the room again, with some kind of wild thought that if I insisted I should find it. 'My window – my window!' I said.

There was one of the professors standing there, and he heard me. 'The window!' said he. 'Ah, you've been taken in with what appears outside. It was put there to be in uniformity with the window on the stair. But it never was a real window. It is just behind that bookcase. Many people are taken in by it,' he said.

His voice seemed to sound from somewhere far away, and as if it would go on for ever; and the hall swam in a dazzle of shining and of noises round me; and the daylight through the open window grew greyer, waiting till it should be over, and the bubble burst.

V

It was Mr Pitmilly who took me home; or rather it was I who took him, pushing him on a little in front of me, holding fast by his arm, not waiting for Aunt Mary or any one. We came out into the daylight again outside, I, without even a cloak or a shawl, with my bare arms, and uncovered head, and the pearls round my neck. There was a rush of the people about, and a baker's boy, that baker's boy, stood right in my way and cried, 'Here's a braw ane!' shouting to the others: the words struck me somehow, as his stone had struck the window, without any reason. But I did not mind the people staring, and hurried across the street, with Mr Pitmilly half a step in advance. The door was open, and Janet standing at it, looking out to see what she could see of the ladies in their grand dresses. She gave a shriek when she saw me hurrying across the street; but I brushed past her, and pushed Mr Pitmilly up the stairs, and took him breathless to the recess, where I threw myself down on the seat, feeling as if I could not have gone another step farther, and waved my hand across to the window. 'There! There!' I cried. Ah! There it was – not that senseless mob – not the theatre and the gas, and the people all in a murmur and clang of talking. Never in all these days had I seen that room so clearly. There was a faint tone of light behind, as if it might have been a reflection from some of those vulgar lights in the hall, and he sat against it, calm, wrapped in his thoughts, with his face turned to the window. Nobody but must have seen him. Janet could have seen him had I called her upstairs. It was like a picture, all the things I knew, and the same attitude, and the atmosphere, full of quietness, not disturbed by anything. I pulled Mr Pitmilly's arm before I let him go, – 'You see, you see!' I cried. He gave me the most bewildered look, as if he would have liked to cry. He saw nothing! I was sure of that from his eyes. He was an old man, and there was no vision in him. If I had called up Janet, she would have seen it all. 'My dear!' he said. "My dear!' waving his hands in a helpless way.

'He has been there all these nights,' I cried, 'and I thought you could tell me who he was and what he was doing; and that he might have taken me in to that room, and showed me, that I might tell papa.

Papa would understand, he would like to hear. Oh, can't you tell me what work he is doing, Mr Pitmilly? He never lifts his head as long as the light throws a shadow, and then when it is like this he turns round and thinks, and takes a rest!'

Mr Pitmilly was trembling, whether it was with cold or I know not what. He said, with a shake in his voice, 'My dear young lady – my dear –' and then stopped and looked at me as if he were going to cry. 'It's peetiful, it's peetiful,' he said; and then in another voice, 'I am going across there again to bring your Aunt Mary home; do you understand, my poor little thing, my – I am going to bring her home – you will be better when she is here.' I was glad when he went away, as he could not see anything: and I sat alone in the dark which was not dark, but quite clear light – a light like nothing I ever saw. How clear it was in that room! not glaring like the gas and the voices, but so quiet, everything so visible, as if it were in another world. I heard a little rustle behind me, and there was Janet, standing staring at me with two big eyes wide open. She was only a little older than I was. I called to her, 'Janet, come here, come here, and you will see him, – come here and see him!' impatient that she should be so shy and keep behind. 'Oh, my bonnie young leddy!' she said, and burst out crying. I stamped my foot at her, in my indignation that she would not come, and she fled before me with a rustle and swing of haste, as if she were afraid. None of them, none of them! not even a girl like myself, with the sight in her eyes, would understand. I turned back again, and held out my hands to him sitting there, who was the only one that knew. 'Oh,' I said, 'say something to me! I don't know who you are, or what you are: but you're lonely and so am I; and I only – feel for you. Say something to me!' I neither hoped that he would hear, nor expected any answer. How could he hear, with the street between us, and his window shut, and all the murmuring of the voices and the people standing about? But for one moment it seemed to me that there was only him and me in the whole world.

But I gasped with my breath, that had almost gone from me, when

I saw him move in his chair! He had heard me, though I knew not how. He rose up, and I rose too, speechless, incapable of anything but this mechanical movement. He seemed to draw me as if I were a puppet moved by his will. He came forward to the window, and stood looking across at me. I was sure that he looked at me. At last he had seen me: at last he had found out that somebody, though only a girl, was watching him, looking for him, believing in him. I was in such trouble and commotion of mind and trembling, that I could not keep on my feet, but dropped kneeling on the window-seat, supporting myself against the window, feeling as if my heart were being drawn out of me. I cannot describe his face. It was all dim, yet there was a light on it: I think it must have been a smile; and as closely as I looked at him he looked at me. His hair was fair, and there was a little quiver about his lips. Then he put his hands upon the window to open it. It was stiff and hard to move; but at last he forced it open with a sound that echoed all along the street. I saw that the people heard it, and several looked up. As for me, I put my hands together, leaning with my face against the glass, drawn to him as if I could have gone out of myself, my heart out of my bosom, my eyes out of my head. He opened the window with a noise that was heard from the West Port to the Abbey. Could any one doubt that?

And then he leaned forward out of the window, looking out. There was not one in the street but must have seen him. He looked at me first, with a little wave of his hand, as if it were a salutation – yet not exactly that either, for I thought he waved me away; and then he looked up and down in the dim shining of the ending day, first to the east, to the old Abbey towers, and then to the west, along the broad line of the street where so many people were coming and going, but so little noise, all like enchanted folk in an enchanted place. I watched him with such a melting heart, with such a deep satisfaction as words could not say; for nobody could tell me now that he was not there, – nobody could say I was dreaming any more. I watched him as if I could not breathe – my heart in my throat, my eyes upon him. He looked up and down, and then he looked back to me. I was the first, and I was the last, though it was not for long: he did know, he did see, who it was that had recognised him and sympathised with him all the time. I was in a kind of rapture, yet stupor too; my look went with his look, following it as if I were his shadow; and then suddenly he was gone, and I saw him no more.

I dropped back again upon my seat, seeking something to support me, something to lean upon. He had lifted his hand and waved it once again to me. How he went I cannot tell, nor where he went I cannot tell; but in a moment he was away, and the window standing open, and the room fading into stillness and dimness, yet so clear, with all its space, and the great picture in its gilded frame upon the wall. It gave me no pain to see him go away. My heart was so content, and I was so worn out and satisfied – for what doubt or question could there be about him now? As I was lying back as weak as water, Aunt Mary came in behind me, and flew to me with a little rustle as if she had come on wings, and put her arms round me, and drew my head on to her breast. I had begun to cry a little, with sobs like a child. 'You saw him, you saw him!' I said. To lean upon her, and feel her so soft, so kind, gave me a pleasure I cannot describe, and her arms round me, and her voice saying 'Honey, my honey!' – as if she were nearly crying too. Lying there I came back to myself, quite sweetly, glad of everything. But I wanted some assurance from them that they had seen him too. I waved my hand to the window that was still standing open, and the room that was stealing away into the faint dark. 'This time you saw it all!' I said, getting more eager. 'My honey!' said Aunt Mary, giving me a kiss: and Mr Pitmilly began to walk about the room with short little steps behind, as if he were out of patience. I sat straight up and put away Aunt Mary's arms. 'You cannot be so blind, so blind!' I cried. 'Oh, not to-night, at least not to-night!' But neither the one nor the other made any reply. I shook myself quite free, and raised myself up. And there, in the middle of the street, stood the baker's boy like a statue, staring up at the open window, with his mouth open and his face full of wonder – breathless, as if he could not believe what he saw. I darted forward, calling to him, and beckoned him to come to me. 'Oh, bring him up! bring him, bring him to me!' I cried.

Mr Pitmilly went out directly, and got the boy by the shoulder. He did not want to come. It was strange to see the little old gentleman, with his beautiful frill and his diamond pin, standing out in the street, with his hand upon the boy's shoulder, and the other boys round, all in a little crowd. And presently they came towards the house, the others all following, gaping and wondering. He came in unwilling, almost resisting, looking as if we meant him some harm. 'Come away, my laddie, come and speak to the young lady,' Mr Pitmilly was saying. And Aunt Mary took my hands to keep me back. But I would not be kept back.

'Boy,' I cried, 'you saw it too: you saw it: tell them you saw it! It is that I want, and no more.'

He looked at me as they all did, as if he thought I was mad. 'What's she wantin' wi' me?' he said; and then, 'I did nae harm, even if I did throw a bit stane at it – and it's nae sin to throw a stane.'

'You rascal!' said Mr Pitmilly, giving him a shake; 'have you been throwing stones? You'll kill somebody some of these days with your stones.' The old gentleman was confused and troubled, for he did not understand what I wanted, nor anything that had happened. And then Aunt Mary, holding my hands and drawing me close to her, spoke. 'Laddie,' she said, 'answer the young lady, like a good lad. There's no intention of finding fault with you. Answer her, my man, and then Janet will give ye your supper before you go.'

'Oh speak, speak!' I cried; 'answer them and tell them! You saw that window opened, and the gentleman look out and wave his hand?'

'I saw nae gentleman,' he said, with his head down, 'except this wee gentleman here.'

'Listen, laddie,' said Aunt Mary. 'I saw ye standing in the middle of the street staring. What were ye looking at?'

'It was naething to make a wark about. It was just yon windy yonder in the library that is nae windy. And it was open – as sure's death.

You may laugh if you like. Is that a' she's wantin' wi' me?'

'You are telling a pack of lies, laddie,' Mr Pitmilly said.

'I'm tellin' nae lees – it was standin' open just like ony ither windy. It's as sure's death. I couldna believe it mysel'; but it's true.'

'And there it is,' I cried, turning round and pointing it out to them with great triumph in my heart. But the light was all grey, it had faded, it had changed. The window was just as it had always been, a sombre break upon the wall.

I was treated like an invalid all that evening, and taken up-stairs to bed, and Aunt Mary sat up in my room the whole night through. Whenever I opened my eyes she was always sitting there close to me, watching. And there never was in all my life so strange a night. When I would talk in my excitement, she kissed me and hushed me like a child. 'Oh, honey, you are not the only one!' she said. 'Oh whisht, whisht, bairn! I should never have let you be there!'

'Aunt Mary, Aunt Mary, you have seen him too?'

'Oh whisht, whisht, honey!' Aunt Mary said: her eyes were shining – there were tears in them. 'Oh whisht, whisht! Put it out of your mind, and try to sleep. I will not speak another word,' she cried.

But I had my arms round her, and my mouth at her ear. 'Who is he there? – tell me that and I will ask no more –'

'Oh honey, rest, and try to sleep! It is just – how can I tell you? – a dream, a dream! Did you not hear what Lady Carnbee said? – the women of our blood –'

'What? what? Aunt Mary, oh Aunt Mary –'

'I canna tell you, ' she cried in her agitation, 'I canna tell you! How can I tell you, when I know just what you know and no more? It is a longing all your life after – it is a looking – for what never comes.'

'He will come,' I cried. 'I shall see him to-morrow – that I know, I know!'

She kissed me and cried over me, her cheek hot and wet like mine. 'My honey, try if you can sleep – try if you can sleep: and we'll wait to see what to-morrow brings.'

'I have no fear,' said I; and then I suppose, though it is strange to think of, I must have fallen asleep – I was so worn-out, and young, and not used to lying in my bed awake. From time to time I opened my eyes, and sometimes jumped up remembering everything: but Aunt Mary was always there to soothe me, and I lay down again in her shelter like a bird in its nest.

But I would not let them keep me in bed next day. I was in a kind of fever, not knowing what I did. The window was quite opaque, without the least glimmer in it, flat and blank like a piece of wood. Never from the first day had I seen it so little like a window. 'It cannot be wondered at,' I said to myself, 'that seeing it like that, and with eyes that are old, not so clear as mine, they should think what they do.' And then I smiled to myself to think of the evening and the long light, and whether he would look out again, or only give me a signal with his hand. I decided I would like that best: not that he should take the trouble to come forward and open it again, but just a turn of his head and a wave of his hand. It would be more friendly and show more confidence, – not as if I wanted that kind of demonstration every night.

I did not come down in the afternoon, but kept at my own window up-stairs alone, till the tea-party should be over. I could hear them making a great talk; and I was sure they were all in the recess staring at the window, and laughing at the silly lassie. Let them laugh! I felt above all that now. At dinner I was very restless, hurrying to get it over; and I think Aunt Mary was restless too. I doubt whether she read her 'Times' when it came; she opened it up so as to shield her, and watched from a corner. And I settled myself in the recess, with my heart full of expectation. I wanted nothing more than to see him writing at his table, and to turn his head and give me a little wave of his hand, just to show that he knew I was there. I sat from half-past seven o'clock to ten o'clock: and the daylight grew softer and softer, till at last it was as if it was shining through a pearl, and not a shadow to be seen. But the window all the time was as black as night, and there was nothing, nothing there.

Well: but other nights it had been like that; he would not be there every night only to please me. There are other things in a man's life, a great learned man like that. I said to myself I was not disappointed. Why should I be disappointed? There had been other nights when he was not there. Aunt Mary watched me, every movement I made, her eyes shining, often wet, with a pity in them that almost made me cry: but I felt as if I were more sorry for her than for myself. And then I flung myself upon her, and asked her, again and again, what it was, and who it was, imploring her to tell me if she knew? and when she had seen him, and what had happened? and what it meant about the women of our blood? She told me that how it was she could not tell, nor when: it was just at the time it had to be; and that we all saw him in our time – 'that is,' she said, 'the ones that are like you and me.' What was it that made her and me different from the rest? But she only shook her head and would not tell me. 'They say,' she said, and then stopped short. 'Oh, honey, try and forget all about it – if I had but known you were of that kind! They say – that once there was one that was a Scholar, and liked his books more than any lady's love. Honey, do not look at me like that. To think I should have brought all this on you!'

'He was a Scholar?' I cried.'And one of us, that must have been a light woman, not like you and me – But maybe it was just in innocence; for who can tell? She waved to him and waved to him to come over: and yon ring was the token: but he would not come. But still she sat at her window and waved and waved – till at last her brothers heard of it, that were stirring men; and then – oh, my honey, let us speak of it no more!'

'They killed him!' I cried, carried away. And then I grasped her with my hands, and gave her a shake, and flung away from her. 'You tell me that to throw dust in my eyes – when I saw him only last night: and he as living as I am, and as young!'

'My honey, my honey!' Aunt Mary said.

After that I would not speak to her for a long time; but she kept close to me, never leaving me when she could help it, and always with that pity in her eyes. For the next night it was the same; and the third night. That third night I thought I could not bear it any longer. I would have to do something – if only I knew what to do! If it would ever get dark, quite dark, there might be something to be done. I had wild dreams of stealing out of the house and getting a ladder, and mounting up to try if I could not open that window, in the middle of the night – if perhaps I could get the baker's boy to help me; and then my mind got into a whirl, and it was as if I had done it; and I could almost see the boy put the ladder to the window, and hear him cry out that there was nothing there. Oh, how slow it was, the night! and how light it was, and everything so clear – no darkness to cover you, no shadow, whether on one side of the street or on the other side! I could not sleep, though I was forced to go to bed. And in the deep midnight, when it is dark dark in every other place, I slipped very softly down-stairs, though there was one board on the landing-place that creaked – and opened the door and stepped out. There was not a soul to be seen, up or down, from the Abbey to the West Port: and the trees stood like ghosts, and the silence was terrible, and everything as clear as day. You don't know what silence is till you find it in the light like that, not morning but night, no sunrising, no shadow, but everything as clear as the day.

It did not make any difference as the slow minutes went on: one o'clock, two o'clock. How strange it was to hear the clocks striking in that dead light when there was nobody to hear them! But it made no difference. The window was quite blank; even the marking of the panes seemed to have melted away. I stole up again after a long time, through the silent house, in the clear light, cold and trembling, with despair in my heart.

I am sure Aunt Mary must have watched and seen me coming back, for after a while I heard faint sounds in the house; and very early, when there had come a little sunshine into the air, she came to my bedside with a cup of tea in her hand; and she, too, was looking like a ghost. 'Are you warm, honey – are you comfortable?' she said. 'It doesn't matter,' said I. I did not feel as if anything mattered; unless if one could get into the dark somewhere – the soft, deep dark that would cover you over and hide you – but I could not tell from what. The dreadful thing was that there was nothing, nothing to look for, nothing to hide from – only the silence and the light.

That day my mother came and took me home. I had not heard she was coming; she arrived quite unexpectedly, and said she had no time to stay, but must start the same evening so as to be in London next day, papa having settled to go abroad. At first I had a wild thought I would not go. But how can a girl say I will not, when her mother has come for her, and there is no reason, no reason in the world, to resist, and no right! I had to go, whatever I might wish or any one might say. Aunt Mary's dear eyes were wet; she went about the house drying them quietly with her handkerchief, but she always said, 'It is the best thing for you, honey – the best thing for you!' Oh, how I hated to hear it said that it was the best thing, as if anything mattered, one more than another! The old ladies were all there in the afternoon, Lady Carnbee looking at me from under her black lace, and the diamond lurking, sending out darts from under her finger. She patted me on the shoulder, and told me to be a good bairn. 'And never lippen to what you see from the window,' she said. 'The eye is deceitful as well as the heart.' She kept patting me on the shoulder, and I felt again as if that sharp wicked stone stung me. Was that what Aunt Mary meant when she said yon ring was the token? I thought afterwards I saw the mark on my shoulder. You will say why? How can I tell why? If I had known, I should have been contented, and it would not have mattered any more.

I never went back to St Rule's, and for years of my life I never again looked out of a window when any other window was in sight. You ask me did I ever see him again? I cannot tell: the imagination is a great deceiver, as Lady Carnbee said: and if he stayed there so long, only to punish the race that had wronged him, why should I ever have seen him again? for I had received my share. But who can tell what happens in a heart that often, often, and so long as that, comes back to do its errand? If it was he whom I have seen again, the anger is gone from him, and he means good and no longer harm to the house of the woman that loved him. I have seen his face looking at me from a crowd. There was one time when I came home a widow from India, very sad, with my little children: I am certain I saw him there among all the people coming to welcome their friends. There was nobody to welcome me, – for I was not expected: and very sad was I, without a face I knew: when all at once I saw him, and he waved his hand to me. My heart leaped up again: I had forgotten who he was, but only that it was a face I knew, and I landed almost cheerfully, thinking here was some one who would help me. But he had disappeared, as he did from the window, with that one wave of his hand.

And again I was reminded of it all when old Lady Carnbee died – an old, old woman – and it was found in her will that she had left me that diamond ring. I am afraid of it still. It is locked up in an old sandal-wood box in the lumber-room in the little old country-house which belongs to me, but where I never live. If any one would steal it, it would be a relief to my mind. Yet I never knew what Aunt Mary meant when she said, 'Yon ring was the token,' nor what it could have to do with that strange window in the old College Library of St Rule's.

Sir David Brewster Invents the Kaleidoscope

He clears the atmosphere of cool St Andrews –
Into dense constellations that revolve
At a hand's turn. From Aberdeen, Lord Byron
Looks on with half of Europe, starry-eyed.
Baudelaire will say modern art's like this,
Brilliant and shifty, a fantastic model
Of how the real will open up, the micro–
Particular, the split, then the expanding
Universe that spills out silent stars
Light years from Scotland. It's a toy –
No copyright, it made the man who made it
No money. Just a universal sold
In Glasgow or Bangkok. With an English friend
Later he helped invent the camera,
Became a friend of Hill and Adamson
Who set up tripods in Fife villages,
Went back to being local, became fact.

A Saltire

Two churnfuls of first milk flushed
across a farmland, night-time sky,
the cross flag juts and fluthers
over a St Andrews bay,
unworked by jibs and rudders,
but undone by small, hard waves, its sheen
mingles, one moment skirting-board grey,
the next the tones of a chic silk stole.

Here, where a saint's bones still knock
in the broth, in current-chiselled troughs
ten fathoms down, where last squibs
of fluorine sea-light
dance off dark hulks of rock,
igniting the shells of sculling shrimps,
kicking their frills from relic to relic,
rolling in a thousand acre feet of swell;

humerus, canine, patella brought to us
at *the north-west ends of the earth*
by Regulus, mad dreaming monk
or money maker,
shipwrecked sailor shivering in his cave,
shaking the salt spray from his hair
and weeping for a handful of bleached,
Greek fingers the bay still crosses for luck.

Translated from the Greek by William L. Lorimer

Andro

Καὶ μετὰ τὸ παραδοθῆναι τὸν Ἰωάννην ἦλθεν ὁ Ἰησοῦς εἰς τὴν Γαλιλαίαν κηρύσσων τὸ εὐαγγέλιον τοῦ Θεοῦ καὶ λέγων ὅτι Πεπλήρωται ὁ καιρὸς καὶ ἤγγικεν ἡ βασιλεία τοῦ Θεοῦ· μετανεῖτε καὶ πιστεύετε ἐν τῷ εὐαγγελίῳ. Καὶ παράγων παρὰ τὴν θάλασσαν τῆς Γαλιλαίας εἶδεν Σίμωνα καὶ Ἀνδρέαν τὸν ἀδελφὸν Σίμωνος ἀμφιβάλλοντας ἐν τῇ θαλάσσῃ· ἦσαν γὰρ ἀλεεῖς. καὶ εἶπεν αὐτοῖς ὁ Ἰησοῦς, Δεῦτε ὀπίσω μου, καὶ ποιήσω ὑμᾶς γενέσθαι ἀλεεῖς ἀνθρώπων. καὶ εὐθὺς ἀφέντες τὰ δίκτυα ἠκολούθησαν αὐτῷ.

Efter John hed been incarcerate, Jesus fuir tae Galilee an there preached the Gospel o God. 'The time hes comed,' he said, 'an the Kíngdom of god is naurhaund: repent ye, an belíeve i the Gospel.'

Ae day he wis gaein alangside the Loch o Galilee, whan he saw Símon an his brither Andro castin their net i the watter – they war fishers tae tredd – an he said til them, 'Come awà efter me, an I s' mak ye men-fishers'; an strecht they quat their nets an fallowt him.

HOMER

Aien Aristeuein

Πηλεὺς μέν ᾧ παιδὶ γέρων ἐπέτελλ' Ἀχιλῆϊ
αἰὲν ἀριστεύειν καὶ ὑπείροχον ἔμμεναι ἄλλων·

Then aged Peleus bade his son Achilles
Always to be the best, bravest of all …

ROBERT FERGUSSON

Sae Blyth, Sae Daft

from *ELEGY on JOHN HOGG, late Porter to the University of ST ANDREWS.*

On einings cauld wi' glee we'd trudge	*evenings*
To heat our shins in Johnny's lodge;	
The de'il ane thought his bum to budge	
Wi' siller on us:	*money*
To claw *het pints* we'd never grudge	*clutch celebratory drinks*
O' MOLATIONIS.	*whisky made from molasses*

Say ye, *red gowns*! that aften here	
Hae toasted bakes to *Kattie*'s beer,	
Gin 'ere thir days hae had their peer,	*If ever those*
Sae blyth, sae daft;	
You'll ne'er again in life's career	
Sit ha'f sae saft.	

RODDY LUMSDEN

The Auld Grey Pantoum

St Sally's bells hang heavy in the silver mirk.
Fisher women knit news at the Leddyheid.
Left thumb tied to right big toe and left to right.
The burgled chest of drawers above the seventeenth.

Fisher women knit news at the Leddyheid.
Townies rumoured to exist across the burn.
The burgled chest of drawers above the seventeenth.
Young Tom rowing in towards the crowd and death.

205

Townies rumoured to exist across the burn.
With flounders frisking in the sand beneath the pier,
Young Tom rows towards the weeping crowd and death.
Cath Cinnaechaidh, the Market, Raisin Monday

When flounders frisk in golden sand beneath the pier.
Hackie, Hackston's Hand and Hand-Me-Down-the-Moon.
Cath Cinnaechaidh, the Market, Raisin Monday
Then Hogmanay bells ring out in the silver mirk.

ANDREW was one of Christ's disciples, and gave his name to the city of St Andrews, legend has it, because some of his bones were brought to Fife by St Regulus (also called St Rule) in the early Middle Ages. William Laughton Lorimer (1885-1967), who became Professor of Greek at the University of St Andrews, made his great translation, *The New Testament in Scots* (Southside, 1983) when he was in his 70s and early 80s. Thanks to the work of his son, who transcribed and edited the manuscripts, it was published after his death.

JAMES MATTHEW BARRIE (1860–1937), author of *Peter Pan*, was born in Kirriemuir in 1860. A novelist, dramatist, and man of letters, he delivered an address as Rector of the University of St Andrews in 1922 on the theme of 'Courage'. In it he reflects not least on the slaughter of young men in World War I.

MEG BATEMAN was born in 1959 and grew up in Edinburgh. Her collections of poetry include *Aotromachd agus dàin eile/ Lightness and other poems* (Polygon, 1997). She is a Senior Lecturer at the Gaelic college, Sabhal Mòr Ostaig, on Skye, and an Honorary Senior Lecturer in the School of English at the University of St Andrews.

JAMES BOSWELL (1740–1795) came from Auchinleck in Ayrshire. Trained as a lawyer, he is most famous for writing the world's greatest biography, his *Life of Samuel Johnson*, published in 1791. Ever anxious about his health, his career, and his Scottishness, he toured Europe and met many leading intellectuals. His *Journal of a Tour to the Hebrides* (1785) contains a detailed account of his 1773 visit to St Andrews with Dr Johnson.

WALTER BOWER (1383–1437) was Abbot of the island of Inchcolm in the Firth of Forth. Educated at the universities of Paris and St Andrews, he helped expand the work of older Scottish historians in what came to be called the *Scotichronicon*, a great chronicle of Scottish history. First published in full in 1759, this Latin work was re-edited with a facing English translation in the late twentieth century by D. E. R. Watt.

GEORGE BUCHANAN (1506-1582), one of the greatest Renaissance Latin poets, was born near Killearn, Stirlingshire, and attended the universities of Paris and St Andrews, where he studied with the philosopher John Major. Tutor to both Mary, Queen of Scots, and to King James VI, Buchanan was also a historian of Scotland and an important political theorist who espoused a doctrine of popular sovereignty – which went down badly with his tutee James VI, who much preferred the Divine Right of Kings. Buchanan's colourful career ranged from teaching the great French essayist Montaigne to being imprisoned by the Lisbon Inquisition. In 1566 he was appointed Principal of St Leonard's College in St Andrews and addressed the question of staff salaries.

ROBERT BURNS (1759–1796) never visited St Andrews. Universally regarded as Scotland's national bard, he addressed more poems to the St Andrews *alumnus* Robert Fergusson than to any other poet. The two men never met, but Burns based several of his poems upon Fergusson's, and described his precursor as 'Heaven-taught'. Burns's *Poems, Chiefly in the Scottish Dialect*, published in Kilmarnock in 1786, established his fame. He also wrote in the English dialect.

JOHN BURNSIDE was born in Fife in 1955 and is now a Reader in the School of English at the University of St Andrews. His many books include the poetry collections *Swimming in the Flood* (Cape, 1997) and *The Asylum Dance* (Cape, 2000), the novels *The Dumb House* (Cape, 1997) and *Living Nowhere* (Cape, 2003), and the short story collection *Burning Elvis* (Cape, 2001). He also writes essays and screenplays.

THOMAS A. CLARK's collections of poetry include *Tormentil and Bleached Bones* (Polygon, 1993). Originally from Greenock, he now lives in Fife. His poems have appeared in many magazines and anthologies in Britain, the US, and continental Europe, as well as in small editions from his own Moschatel Press.

ROBERT CRAWFORD was born in Bellshill, Lanarkshire, in 1959, and has lived in St Andrews since 1989. His *Selected Poems* was published by Cape in 2005 and he is co-editor of *The New Penguin Book of Scottish Verse* (2000). He is Professor of Modern Scottish Literature at the University of St Andrews.

ANNA CROWE comes originally from Plymouth and now lives in St Andrews. A poet, translator, and creative-writing tutor, she has served as Artistic Director of StAnza, Scotland's poetry festival. Her collections of poetry include *Skating Out of the House* (Peterloo, 1997) and *A Secret History of Rhubarb* (Mariscat Press, 2004).

MEAGHAN DELAHUNT grew up in Australia, studied at the University of Melbourne, and is now a Lecturer in English at the University of St Andrews where she teaches creative writing. Her first novel, *In the Blue House* was published by Bloomsbury in 2001. She is now completing her second novel, *The Prayer Wheel*, and is working on a collection of short stories.

WALTER DE LA MARE (1873–1976) was a poet as well as a novelist, short-story writer, and critic. His books include *The Listeners* (1912) and his *Collected Poems* was published by Faber in 1979. De la Mare has a particular fondness for the spectral and haunted. He was awarded an honorary DLitt by the University of St Andrews in 1923 and is buried in St Paul's Cathedral.

GAVIN DOUGLAS (c. 1474–1522) was educated at the University of St Andrews and became Bishop of Dunkeld. His *Eneados*, a translation into Scots of Virgil's *Aeneid*, is one of the first translations of a classical epic into a modern European vernacular language. Each of its thirteen books has an original prologue by Gavin Douglas; in the extract from the prologue to Book VII in this anthology 'Eolus' is Aeolus, ruler of the winds, an appropriately St Andrean minor deity.

WILLIAM DRUMMOND OF HAWTHORNDEN (1585–1649) was a friend of Arthur Johnston (see below) and of Sir John Scott of Scotstarvit, after whom the St Andrews University Chair of Latin is named. The first Scottish poet to produce a body of highly accomplished poetry in English, Drummond is also the probable author of the macaronic Latin and English poem, the 'Polemo-Middinia' or 'The Midden-Battle between Lady Scotstarvit and the Mistress of Newbarns' in which, among many other things, Lady Scotstarvit lets off a fart as loud as the blast of the famous cannon, Mons Meg. As Drummond knew, the Scottish Parliament sat in Parliament Hall, South Street, St Andrews, in 1645–6 when there was plague in Edinburgh.

WILLIAM DUNBAR lived from around 1460 to 1520. One of the greatest of the early Renaissance Scottish Makars, his virtuoso poetry extends from the bawdy to the religious. He is thought to have studied at the University of St Andrews in the late 1470s, before travelling in Europe and working at the court of King James IV of Scotland. 'Sanct Salvatour' is a title given to Jesus, and is cognate with the name of St Salvator's College.

DOUGLAS DUNN was born in Inchinnan, Renfrewshire, in 1942. His collections of poetry include *Terry Street* (Faber, 1969), *St Kilda's Parliament* (Faber, 1981), *Elegies* (Faber, 1985), and *The Year's Afternoon* (Faber, 2000). His *New Selected Poems* was published by Faber in 2003. In

1991 he was appointed Professor of English at the University of St Andrews, after a term as Writer in Residence. In 1993 he became Director of the University of St Andrews School of English's highly successful MLitt in Creative Writing, the first of its kind in Scotland.

ROBERT FERGUSSON (1750–1774) signed his name as 'Rob' when he matriculated as a student at the University of St Andrews in 1765. During his three years in St Andrews he was popular with some students, but detested by others, one of whom wrote in a library book that he was 'a snake in human form stain'd with infamy and wickedness'. He died in Edinburgh's madhouse at the age of twenty-four after writing some of the best poems made in eighteenth-century Scotland. In 2000 the University of St Andrews Scottish Studies Institute commissioned a garland of poems in Fergusson's memory, and ran a series of lectures published by Tuckwell Press in 2003 as *'Heaven-Taught Fergusson': Robert Burns's Favourite Scottish Poet*. By a pleasant irony of history, his statue now graces the office of the Principal of the University of St Andrews.

LILLIAS SCOTT FORBES is the last surviving member of the group of Scottish Nationalist intellectuals, writers and artists who came to St Andrews in the 1930s at the time when the magazine *The Modern Scot* was edited from the town. Author of memoirs of her father, the composer Francis George Scott, and of other friends such as Willa and Edwin Muir, she is a poet, essayist, and dramatist whose home is in St Andrews.

BENJAMIN FRANKLIN (1706–1790) was born in Boston, but spent a good deal of his life in Philadelphia and in Europe. His celebrated *Autobiography* was published in 1793 and is a classic of American culture. While it was his scientific work on lightning and electricity which led to the award of his honorary degree from the University of St

Andrews in 1759, he is one of several St Andrews graduates involved in the drafting and signing of the American Declaration of Independence.

LINDA GREGERSON teaches English and creative writing at the University of Michigan, Ann Arbor. Her third collection of poetry, *Waterborne*, was published by Houghton Mifflin in 2002. 'Half Light' was written following a visit to St Andrews to read her work to creative writing students in the University's School of English.

SARAH HALL was born in Cumbria in 1974. After studying on the MLitt in Creative Writing in the School of English at the University of St Andrews, she published her first novel *Haweswater* (Faber, 2002). Her second novel, *The Electric Michelangelo* (Faber) was shortlisted for the 2004 Man Booker Prize.

SEAMUS HEANEY was born in County Derry, Northern Ireland, in 1939 and awarded the Nobel Prize for Literature in 1995. Among his collections of poetry are *Death of a Naturalist* (1966), *Field Work* (1979), and *Seeing Things* (1991). In 1996 for the St Andrews Scottish Studies Institute he delivered one in the series of Robert Burns Bicentenary Lectures which were later published as *Robert Burns and Cultural Authority* (Polygon, 1999). In 1999 for the School of English he delivered the George Jack Memorial Lecture in St Andrews. He was awarded an honorary degree of DLitt by the University of St Andrews in 2005.

W. N. HERBERT was born in Dundee in 1961. His collections of poetry in Scots and English include *Forked Tongue* (Bloodaxe, 1994), *Cabaret McGonagall* (Bloodaxe, 1996), and *The Big Bumper Book of Troy* (Bloodaxe, 2002). Other books include a study of Hugh MacDiarmid (OUP, 1992), and the anthology of poets' writing about poetry, *Strong Words*, co-edited with Matthew Hollis (Bloodaxe, 2000). He teaches creative writing at the University of Newcastle-upon-Tyne.

HOMER is traditionally credited as the author of the Greek epic poems *The Iliad* and *The Odyssey*. Several cities have competed for the honour of having been his birthplace, but none of them is St Andrews. Lines from Books VI and XI of *The Iliad* contain the phrase 'aien aristeuein' (always to be the best) which were adopted by the University of St Andrews as its motto in 1773 (when Boswell and Johnson visited), if not before.

ANDREW B. JACKSON was born in Glasgow in 1965, grew up in Bramhall, Cheshire, and received his secondary education at Bell Baxter High School in Cupar, before going to the University of Edinburgh. His first collection of poetry, *Fire Stations*, was published by Anvil in 2003. He lives in Glasgow.

KATHLEEN JAMIE was born in Johnstone, Renfrewshire, in 1962, and studied Philosophy at the University of Edinburgh. She is a Reader in English at the University of St Andrews, where she teaches creative writing and Scottish literature. Her *Selected Poems* appeared from Bloodaxe in 2002 with the title *Mr and Mrs Scotland are Dead* and her most recent collection is *The Tree House* (Picador, 2004). Her prose books include *Among Muslims* (Sort of Books, 2002) and *Findings* (Sort of Books, 2005).

KAY REDFIELD JAMISON's books include *Night Falls Fast: Understanding Suicide* (Knopf, 1999) and *Exuberance* (Knopf, 2004). She is Professor of Psychiatry at the Johns Hopkins University School of Medicine, and an Honorary Professor in the School of English, University of St Andrews. In her autobiography, *An Unquiet Mind* (Picador, 1997), she writes about her time as a Junior Year Abroad student in St Andrews.

SAMUEL JOHNSON (1709–84) was an English man of letters whose greatest achievements include his *Dictionary* (1755) and his *Lives of the English Poets* (1779–81). Immortalised by his Scottish biographer, James Boswell, Johnson visited St Andrews in 1773 with Boswell as part of their Scottish tour; this was written up in Johnson's *A Journey to the Western Isles of Scotland* (1775). Johnson was notorious for Scotophobic remarks: his *Dictionary* famously defines the word 'oats' as 'A grain, which in England is generally given to horses, but in Scotland supports the people.' Robert Fergusson refers to this definition in his poem 'To the Principal and Professors of the University of St Andrews'.

ARTHUR JOHNSTON (1587–1641) was born in Inverurie and, after study in Aberdeen, spent much of his life on continental Europe before becoming Lord Rector of King's College, Aberdeen, in 1632. With Sir John Scott of Scotstarvit Tower, near St Andrews, he edited the great anthology of Scottish Latin poets, the *Delitiae Poetarum Scotorum* (1637). Arthur Johnston is one of Scotland's finest Latin poets, and 'Andreapolis' is probably the best of the series of *Encomia Urbium* in which he hymns Scottish towns from Inverurie to Glasgow.

JOHN JOHNSTON was born in Aberdeen around 1568. Like his kinsman, Arthur Johnston, he studied in continental Europe before returning to Scotland where he took up a teaching position at the University of St Andrews around 1593. His Latin epigrams show him at his most elegant, and he produced a series of short poems on distinguished Scots, including the Reformation Protestant martyrs Patrick Hamilton and George Wishart, as well as other figures associated with St Andrews such as John Knox and John Winram. He died in St Andrews in 1611.

BRIAN JOHNSTONE is the founding Director of StAnza, Scotland's poetry festival, which is run in St Andrews by local people each year with support from the University and other sponsors. A former

St Andrews student, his collections of poetry include *The Lizard Silence*, published by Scottish Cultural Press.

A. L. KENNEDY was born in Dundee in 1967. Her novels include *Everything You Need* (Cape, 1999) and *Paradise* (Cape, 2004); her short story collections include *Indelible Acts* (Cape, 2002). She once posed patiently to be photographed in front of the large statue of St Andrew in St Andrews Botanic Gardens, and is a Lecturer in the School of English, University of St Andrews, where she teaches creative writing.

RUDYARD KIPLING (1865–1936) was born in Bombay. Author of *Plain Tales from the Hills* (1888), *The Jungle Book* (1894), *Kim* (1901) and other prose fiction as well as many collections of poems, he was installed as Rector of St Andrews University on 10 October 1923. Awarded the Nobel Prize for Literature in 1907, Kipling is the subject of an intellectual biography by the modern St Andrews academic Phillip Mallett.

JOHN KNOX (c. 1513–1572), a central figure in the Scottish Reformation, is thought to have studied at the University of St Andrews under the philosopher John Major, and was among the Protestant forces besieged in St Andrews Castle in 1547. When the castle fell to the French, he was captured and made a galley slave. An ardent Protestant, Knox attacked Mary Tudor of England in *The First Blast of the Trumpet against the Monstrous Regiment of Women* (1556), and encouraged her subjects to overthrow her. Back in Scotland, he wrote up his own exploits and those of his compatriots in his often vivid *History of the Reformation of Religion within the Realm of Scotland*, completed in 1586. Not without self-aggrandisement, Knox writes of himself in the third person.

ANDREW LANG (1844–1912) was born in Selkirk, and started writing poetry as a St Andrews undergraduate in the early 1860s. Though a good deal of his time was spent in Oxford and London, where he was a leading man of letters, he lived in St Andrews towards the end of his life, and published a history of the place in 1893. A close friend of R. L. Stevenson, Lang was a polymath whose publications ranged from poetry through golf to history and anthropology, though he may be best remembered for his 'fairy books' for children. Lang's poem 'Almae Matres' is said to recall his St Andrews student friend Henry Brown, who died young.

LIZ LOCHHEAD was born in Motherwell in 1947 and studied at the Glasgow School of Art. She has lived in the United States, Canada, and Turkey, though her home is now in Glasgow. Her plays include *Mary Queen of Scots Got Her Head Chopped Off* (Penguin, 1989) and translations of Moliere's comedies into Scots. Her collections of poetry include *The Colour of Black and White* (Polygon, 2003). She holds an honorary DLitt from the University of St Andrews.

RODDY LUMSDEN was born in St Andrews in 1966 and schooled at Madras College. After studying at the University of Edinburgh, and working as Writer in Residence for the City of Aberdeen, he moved south, and now lives in Bristol. His collections of poetry include *Yeah Yeah Yeah* (Bloodaxe, 1997) and *The Book of Love* (Bloodaxe, 2000), as well as the pamphlet of St Andrews poems *The Bubble Bride*.

DAVID LYNDSAY, often styled and spelled Sir David Lindsay of the Mount (a Fife estate near Cupar), was born around 1490. He probably studied at the University of St Andrews, and was active in the courts of King James IV and James V of Scotland. Though he wrote many fine poems, he is best remembered for his great Reformation drama, *Ane Satyre of the Thrie Estaitis* (1553), performed in Cupar; his poem, 'The Tragedie of the Cardinall' (1547) has Cardinal Beaton's ghost speak an almost Browningesque monologue. Lyndsay died in 1555.

HUGH MacDIARMID (1892–1978) was born in Langholm, in the Scottish Borders, and was the leading figure of the Scottish Renaissance cultural movement, as well as being a founder of the National Party of Scotland. His most famous Scots poems include the lyrics of *Sangschaw* (1925) and *Penny Wheep* (1926) as well as *A Drunk Man Looks at the Thistle* (1926); his finest extended poem in English, 'On a Raised Beach', is dedicated to the St Andrews Scottish Nationalist intellectual James H. Whyte, who ran the Abbey Bookshop. When he was planning his Scottish Renaissance just after World War I, MacDiarmid and his wife lived briefly in a house in Market Street, St Andrews, which was later demolished to make way for the University's Buchanan Building.

JAMES MELVILL (1556–1614) was a student at St Leonard's College, St Andrews, from 1571 until 1574, and later became a Professor at St Mary's College. As a first-year student 'because I understood nocht the regent's language in teatching, . . . I did nothing but bursted and grat [cried and sobbed]'. His *Autobiography and Diary*, edited by Robert Pitcairn for the Wodrow Society in 1842, provides an intimate account of his life and times.

EDWIN MORGAN was born in 1920 and studied at the University of Glasgow, where he later bacame a Professor of English. Following the publication of his *Collected Poems* (Carcanet, 1990), he was appointed Scotland's first National Poet. Among many honours, he holds a DLitt from the University of St Andrews. He is a writer of remarkable range whose work includes sound poems, concrete poems, and experimental works as well as powerful monologues and sonnet sequences such as *Sonnets from Scotland* (1984), from which the poem in this book is taken.

EDWIN MUIR (1887-1959) was born in Orkney. A poet, novelist, critic and autobiographer, he was living in St Andrews when he published his most controversial prose book, *Scott and Scotland*, in 1936. His *Collected Poems* was published by Faber in 1960, and T. S. Eliot edited his *Selected*

Poems in 1965. In the mid-1930s Muir and his wife Willa lived opposite St Andrews Castle in the house called Castlelea, on the Scores, close to what is now The Poetry House. His academic appointments included the wardenship of Newbattle Abbey College, and the Charles Eliot Norton professorship at Harvard. His autobiography is a classic of modern Scottish prose.

WILLA MUIR (1890–1970) studied Classics at the University of St Andrews and returned to live, not entirely happily, in the town in the 1930s. Her novels include *Imagined Corners* (1931), and *Mrs Ritchie* (1933); for Virginia and Leonard Woolf at the Hogarth Press she wrote *Women: An Inquiry* (1925), which was followed by her feminist study *Mrs Grundy in Scotland* (1936). She was largely responsible for translating Kafka's *The Castle* into English, wrote an insightful book on ballads, and published her autobiographical memoir *Belonging* in 1968. There is an important collection of her papers in St Andrews University Library.

PAUL MULDOON was born in Moy, County Armagh, Northern Ireland, in 1951. Educated at the Queen's University, Belfast, he worked for the BBC in Northern Ireland until 1985. He lives in Princeton, New Jersey, where he is Howard G. B. Clark Professor of the Humanities at Princeton University. He is also an Honorary Professor in the School of English, University of St Andrews. His *Poems 1968–1998* was published by Faber in 2001, and followed by Moy *Sand and Gravel* (Faber, 2002).

LES MURRAY was born in rural New South Wales in 1938 and still lives there. Widely regarded as Australia's greatest poet, his collections of poetry include *The People's Otherworld* (1983) and *Translations from the Natural World* (Carcanet, 1992). Of Scottish descent, Murray grew up hearing Burns recited, and has spent a good deal of time in Scotland. In 2000 he read his poem in memory of Robert Fergusson along with an array of Scottish poets in the Younger Hall, St Andrews.

ROBERT FULLER MURRAY (1863–1894) was born in Roxbury, Massachusetts, the son of a Unitarian minister. He was an undergraduate at St Andrews University from 1881 until 1885, after which he worked as a journalist and poet. His collection of poems *The Scarlet Gown* (1891) includes a number of very nostalgic works about St Andrews and his student days.

MARGARET OLIPHANT (1828–1897) was born in Wallyford, East Lothian, though she spent much of her life in England and continental Europe. She published over a hundred books, including her *Chronicles of Carlingford* and a number of novels such as *Effie Ogilvie* (1886) and *Kirsteen* (1890) which are set in Scotland. A historian, critic, and biographer, she was a close friend of the wife of John Tulloch, Principal of St Mary's College, and wrote his biography. She enjoyed visiting St Andrews throughout her life. Some of her best work is in her ghost stories of the 1880s and 1890s.

JAY PARINI is Axinn Professor of English at Middlebury College in Vermont. He is a poet, novelist, critic and biographer whose collections of poetry include *Anthracite Country* (Random House 1982). His prose books include *The Art of Teaching* (OUP, 2005) in which he writes about his time in St Andrews.

DON PATERSON was born in Dundee in 1963. His collections of poetry include *Nil Nil* (Faber, 1993), *God's Gift to Women* (Faber, 1997), *The Eyes* (Faber, 1999), and *Landing Light* (Faber, 2003). A musician, anthologist, and wit, he holds a Lectureship in the School of English, University of St Andrews, where he teaches creative writing, poetry and Scottish Studies.

TOM POW was born in Edinburgh in 1950. He studied English at St Andrews University, and now teaches creative writing at Glasgow

University's Crichton Campus in Dumfries. His collections of poetry include *Rough Seas* (Canongate, 1987), *The Moth Trap* (Canongate, 1990), and *Landscapes and Legacies* (inyx, 2003).

IAN RANKIN was born in Fife in 1960. His novels include *Black and Blue* (Orion, 1997), *Set in Darkness* (Orion, 2000), and *A Question of Blood* (Orion, 2003). His Inspector Rebus novels have made him one of the leading crime writers in the English-speaking world, and he was awarded an honorary DLitt from the University of St Andrews in 2001. In *Set in Darkness* Rebus visits St Andrews: 'He knew it represented something extraordinary, but couldn't have said what. The words didn't quite exist.'

ALASTAIR REID was born in Whithorn, Wigtonshire, in 1926, and studied English at the University of St Andrews before going on to a long career as a staff writer on the *New Yorker* magazine. A selection of his essays and poems was published by Canongate in 1987 under the title *Whereabouts: Notes on being a Foreigner*. Among the visitors Reid brought to St Andrews was his friend Jorge Luis Borges, who recited Scottish ballads; Reid was present at the launch of The Poetry House in St Andrews in 2002, when he held a large balloon.

ROBIN ROBERTSON grew up in the north east of Scotland and now works as an editor for the publisher Jonathan Cape. His collections of poetry include *A Painted Field* (Picador, 1997) and *Slow Air* (Picador, 2002). He lives in London.

STEPHEN SCOBIE was born in 1943, grew up in Fife, and studied English at the University of St Andrews, before emigrating to Canada where he is now Professor of English at the University of Victoria, British Columbia. His book *The Spaces in Between: Selected Poems 1965–2001* was published by NeWest Press, Edmonton, in 2003, when he also returned to St Andrews to read at St Anza.

TOM SCOTT (1918–1995) was born in Glasgow but grew up in St Andrews where his father worked as a builder's labourer. Tom Scott's Scots versions of Villon were admired by T. S. Eliot and his collections of poetry include *The Ship and Ither Poems* (1963) and *Collected Shorter Poems* (Agenda/Chapman Publications, 1993). Scott's sequence of St Andrews poems 'Brand the Builder' (1975) celebrates the local working people of St Andrews, and shows a clear dislike of those with pretensions to be 'gentry'. Though he celebrated Professor D'Arcy Thomson, Scott detested the university, seeing it as 'an anglicisit travesty o itsel' whose 'heichest aim, its circle-squarin glory,/ Is first-class brains that nanetheless vote Tory.' In the 1970s the University of St Andrews was associated with several of the ideologues of Thatcherism.

WALTER SCOTT (1771–1832), Scotland's greatest and most influential novelist, was educated in Edinburgh where the main railway station is named after his first novel, *Waverley* (1814). His other historical novels include *Rob Roy* (1818), *The Heart of Midlothian* (1818), and *Ivanhoe* (1820). His career as a novelist was preceded by a hugely successful career as the poet of *The Lay of the Last Minstrel* and other works. He built the remarkable house of Abbotsford, in his native Scottish Borders. Though Scott did not marry Williamina Belsches, whose name he carved on the turf at St Andrews Castle, she later became the mother of a Principal of the University of St Andrews, J. D. Forbes.

SUSAN SELLERS won a Canongate Prize for New Writing in 2002 and is completing her first novel. Her academic books include *Myth and Fairytale in Contemporary Women's Fiction* (Palgrave, 2001). She is Professor of English and Related Literature at the University of St Andrews and General Editor of the St Andrews/Dundee Research Edition of Virginia Woolf, to be published by Cambridge University Press.

ROBERT LOUIS STEVENSON (1850–1894) wrote several of Scotland's finest novels, including *Treasure Island* (1883), *Kidnapped* (1885), and *The Strange Case of Dr Jekyll and Mr Hyde* (1886). His essay 'The Coast of Fife' recalls a visit he made to St Andrews as a youngster of thirteen, accompanying his father, a great lighthouse engineer. They found the state of the harbour lights 'pitiable', then crossed Magus Muir which Stevenson associated with the assassination of Archbishop Sharpe of St Andrews. He writes about 'the live bum-bee that flew out of Sharpe's 'bacco-box, thus clearly indicating his complicity with Satan'.

WILLIAM TENNANT (1784–1848) was born in Anstruther, and studied at the University of St Andrews, where he later became Professor of Oriental Languages. His poem 'Anster Fair' probably influenced Byron's *Don Juan*, and his account of the Reformation assault on St Andrews Cathedral, 'Papistry Storm'd' has considerable comic brio; few, however, remember his 1823 verse drama, *Cardinal Beaton*.

DOUGLAS YOUNG (1913–1973) was a student at the University of St Andrews, and later taught Greek there before taking up a chair at the University of North Carolina, Chapel Hill. A committed Scottish Nationalist, Young was a good friend of the Gaelic poet Sorley MacLean; he refused conscription during World War II, and was imprisoned in Edinburgh Castle where he translated Psalm XXIII into Scots. A Scots-language poet and dramatist who translated Aristophanes's *Frogs* as *The Puddocks* (1957) and the same Greek dramatist's *Birds* as *The Burdies* for the Edinburgh International Festival in 1966, Young is author of the classic account, *St Andrews: Town and Gown, Royal and Ancient* (1969). He is one of the few St Andrews classicists to have been driven away in the back of a black maria.

J. M. Barrie: from *Courage* (Hodder & Stoughton, 1922).

Walter Bower: from *Scotichronicon: Volume 8*, edited by D. E. R. Watt (The Mercat Press, 1987), reprinted by permission of University of St Andrews.

John Burnside: 'History', from *The Light Trap* (Jonathan Cape, 2002), reprinted by permission of the author and The Random House Group Ltd.

Robert Crawford: 'St Andrews' translated from the Latin of Arthur Johnston, 'D'Arcy', 'St Andrews', 'Sir David Brewster Invents the Kaleidoscope', from *Selected Poems* (Cape, 2005), reprinted with permission.

Walter de la Mare: 'A Memory', from *St Andrews* (A. & C. Black, 1926), reprinted by permission of The Literary Trustees of Walter de la Mare and the Society of Authors as their representative.

Douglas Dunn: from 'Body Echoes', in *Dante's Drum-kit* (Faber & Faber, 1993), reprinted by permission of the author and publisher.

Linda Gregerson: 'Half Light' from *Waterborne* (NY: Houghton Mifflin, 2002), reprinted by permission of the author and publisher.

W. N. Herbert: 'The Well' from *Sharawaggi* (Polygon, 1990), reprinted with permission.

Kay Redfield Jamison: extract from *An Unquiet Mind* (Picador, 1997), reprinted by permission of Pan Macmillan, London, UK.

Brian Johnstone: 'The March Stone' from *Homing* (Lobby Press, 2004), reprinted by permission of the author.

Rudyard Kipling: 'A Rector's Memory', from *St Andrews* (A. & C. Black, 1926), reprinted by permission of A. P. Watt Ltd on behalf of The National Trust for Places of Historic Interest or Natural Beauty.

Liz Lochhead: 'Construction For A Site: Library On An Old Croquet Lawn, St Andrews. Nine Approaches', from *Dreaming Frankenstein & Collected Poems* (Polygon, 1984), reprinted by permission of the publisher.

William L. Lorimer: from *The New Testament in Scots*, first published in 2001 in Great Britain by Canongate Books Ltd., 14 High Street, Edinburgh, EH1 1TE, reprinted by permission of the publisher.

Roddy Lumsden: 'A Saltire', 'The Auld Grey Pantoum', 'The Designer's Dream', from *The Bubble Bride* (St Andrews Bay, 2003), reprinted by permission of St Andrews Bay Golf Resort & Spa; 'The Drop of a Hat', from *Roddy Lumsden is Dead* (Wrecking Ball Press, 2001), reprinted by permission of the publisher.

Hugh MacDiarmid: from *The Raucle Tongue: Selected Essays, Journalism & Interviews: Volume 2*, edited by Angus Calder, Glen Murray and Alan Riach (Carcanet Press, 1997), reprinted by permission of the publisher.

Edwin Morgan: 'Thomas Young, M. A. (St Andrews)', from *Collected Poems* (Carcanet Press, 1990), reprinted by permission of the publisher.

Edwin Muir: 'The Castle', from *The Complete Poems of Edwin Muir*, edited by P. H. Butter (Association for Scottish Literary Studies, 1991), reprinted by permission of Faber & Faber Ltd.

Willa Muir: from *Belonging: A Memoir* (The Hogarth Press, 1968).

Les Murray: 'Robert Fergusson Night' from R. Crawford, ed., *Heaven-Taught Fergusson* (Tuckwell, 2003) and *Poems the Size of Photographs* (Carcanet, 2002), reprinted by permission of the author.

Jay Parini: extract from *The Art of Teaching* (Oxford University Press, 2005), reprinted by permission of the publisher.

Ian Rankin: 'Back from the Beach' from *The Scotsman* Weekend section, 16 January 1999, reprinted by permission of the author.

Alastair Reid: extracts from 'Digging up Scotland' from *Whereabouts* (Canongate, 1987) reprinted by permission of the author.

Robin Robertson: 'Mayday 1997' from *Verse*, reprinted by permission of the author.

Stephen Scobie: 'The Corner of Abbey Street and Greenside Place' from *The Spaces in Between* (NeWest Press, Edmonton, 2003), reprinted by permission of the author.

Tom Scott: from 'Brand the Builder', in *The Collected Shorter Poems of Tom Scott* (*Agenda*/Chapman Publications, 1993), reprinted by permission of *Agenda*.

Douglas Young: extracts from Clara Young, David Murison, eds., *A Clear Voice: Douglas Young, Poet and Polymath* (Loanhead: Macdonald, 1977), reprinted by permission of Clara Young.

The publisher apologizes for any errors or omissions in the above list and would be grateful to be notified of any corrections that should be incorporated in any reprint of this volume. Some extracts in this book have been given new, individual titles.

INDEX OF AUTHORS